Social Origins of Religion

Social Origins of Religion

Roger Bastide

Translated by Mary Baker
Foreword by James L. Peacock

University of Minnesota Press
Minneapolis • London

The University of Minnesota Press gratefully acknowledges financial assistance provided by the French Ministry of Culture for the translation of this book.

Originally published as *Éléments de sociologie religieuse* in 1935 by Armand Colin; copyright 1997 Éditions Stock.

Published by the University of Minnesota Press
111 Third Avenue South, Suite 290
Minneapolis, MN 55401-2520
http://www.upress.umn.edu

Library of Congress Cataloging-in-Publication Data

Bastide, Roger, 1898–1974.
  [Éléments de sociologie religieuse. English]
  Social origins of religion / Roger Bastide ; translated by Mary Baker; foreword by James L. Peacock.
    p.   cm.
  Includes bibliographical references and index.
  ISBN 0-8166-3248-0 (alk. paper) — ISBN 0-8166-3249-9 (pbk. : alk. paper)
  1. Religion and sociology.   I. Title.
  BL60 .B313   2003
  210—dc21   2003010209

Printed in the United States of America on acid-free paper

The University of Minnesota is an equal-opportunity educator and employer.

12 11 10 09 08 07 06 05 04 03   10 9 8 7 6 5 4 3 2 1

Contents

Foreword

James L. Peacock

Roger Bastide's *Éléments de sociologie religieuse*, translated here as *Social Origins of Religion*, was published in 1935. It appeared early in his career, shortly after *Les Problèmes de la vie mystique* (Problems of the mystical life, published in 1931) and preceding works on psychoanalysis, art, Haiti, African religions in Brazil, and Africa in the New World, all to be published during the next half century.

A first clue to the context and significance of this work is given by its date of publication and its bibliography. It was published not long after World War I had intervened between the grand theories of religion that characterized the late nineteenth and early twentieth centuries and the narrowing, fieldwork-based focus that came after World War I. Bastide is positioned between these two watersheds. He refers to path-setting studies by Émile Durkheim and Sigmund Freud, secondarily to Max Weber and Karl Marx. The anthropology he invokes is especially the vast comparative work of Sir James Frazer: Frazer's *Golden Bough* marked the era just before the flood of ethnographic studies was unleashed by Bronislaw Malinowski's field-work in the Trobriands during World War I. Malinowski's career was inspired by *The Golden Bough*, which his mother read to him in Kraków, propelling him from mathematics and physics to anthropology—a conversion he apparently made while delirious from a fever. Having converted, Malinowski then led the charge to topple his idol, Frazer, and convert anthropology from grand evolutionary theory to fieldwork. Malinowski's fieldwork among the Trobriands does not enter Bastide's discussion, though he does refer briefly to his work in Australia.

Bastide's cornerstone is Durkheim, to which this book is a reaction, sequel, and critique; Durkheim's *Elementary Forms of Religious Life* was published in 1912, and Durkheim's thesis that the religious is a projection of social life is echoed not only in Bastide's title but also immediately in his thesis, which in part is an argument with Durkheim. Freud is introduced almost immediately, too, if only to be dismissed as psychological, hence marginal to a work on the sociological aspect of religion. Weber is referenced specifically by his *Afsätze zur Religionsoziologie*, his collected works on the sociology of religion, which were later to be translated by Talcott Parsons and others as *The Protestant Ethic and the Spirit of Capitalism, Religion of India, Religion of China*, and *Ancient Judaism*. While Weber is not introduced as part of Bastide's overriding framework and other German writers, such as Friedrich Schleiermacher, are deemed too narrowly Christian for the comparative scope of Bastide's study, one might suspect that the mystical and individual dimension that he relishes in counterpoint to Durkheim's sociologism was enriched by the Germans as well as by the cognitive psychologies of Frazer and other British writers such as Tylor.

Returning to Durkheim, it is worth asking how Bastide fits or does not fit into the Durkheimian genealogy, passing through Marcel Mauss, Henri Hubert, and Robert Hertz to Claude Lévi-Strauss and on to postmodernism.

What is striking is how this work deviates creatively from this lineage. While this is a very "French" work, it returns to a source before Durkheim—Auguste Comte—thus embracing a vision of cultural evolution and an interest in history and change. While this dimension is present in Durkheim and his followers, the fundamental emphasis in Durkheim and among Durkheimians through Lévi-Strauss is on constancy and structure: the emphasis continues from Durkheim's elementary forms of religion to Lévi-Strauss's elementary structures of kinship, and it is captured by famous aphorisms such as that of Lévi-Strauss in his debate with Jean-Paul Sartre: "History, like many careers, can lead anywhere provided you get out of it." Like Durkheim, Lévi-Strauss seeks the structure underlying seeming change. Bastide prefers Henri Bergson's more fluid sense of life as an ever flowing stream, and he is open to history and change. Thus, Bastide refuses Durkheim's exclusive focus on "primitive" religion as an elementary form explaining all later ones, and he embraces the study of changes, including contemporary religious movements.

Roger Bastide was born in Nîmes on April 1, 1898, to parents who taught at a Protestant primary school. Bastide may have been a precociously religious child, after a fashion: he confided to a friend that as a young boy, he would cut insects in two and bury them in a ritual manner. After early education at the school where his parents taught, Bastide entered the local lycée at age ten and earned a scholarship to prepare for the École Normale Supérieure at the lycée Lakanal de Sceaux in 1915.

The First World War intervened in Bastide's education in 1916, and he left for Valence for military service. While stationed in Valence, Bastide studied for a philosophy degree at nearby Grenoble. Sent to the front as a telegrapher in 1917, Bastide was not able to resume his studies until 1919, when he entered the University of Bordeaux.

In Bordeaux Bastide began writing poems and seriously reading André Gide, Marcel Proust, and Pierre Jean Jouve. For his degree in philosophy, he presented a paper titled "La Renaissance du cynisme à Rome au Ier siècle avant J-C" (The renaissance of cynicism in Rome in the first century B.C.). Bastide studied under Gaston Richard, Durkheim's successor at Bordeaux, and became a fan of Richard and of Raoul Allier. Bastide published his first article in 1921, "Patronat social et christianisme sociale" (Social employment and social Christianity) in the Protestant journal *Le Christianisme Social*. Three texts followed in the next year, one on poetry, the others on Protestantism.

After passing another graduate exam (the *concours d'Agrégation*) in 1924, Bastide was appointed to a post at Cahors and elected to municipal office. He married in 1926 and had a daughter the same year. He began publishing again in 1927, with two articles on the writer André Lamandé printed in *Le Quercy*, a local paper run by his father-in-law. After also publishing more poetry, Bastide began a prolific output of academic writing in the next year, publishing twelve texts. Most notably in 1928, he wrote *Marcel Proust et le pilpoul*, on Proust and Judaism (*pilpoul*, or *poivre fort*, strong pepper, is a term for detailed discussion and study—of each word in some cases—of the Torah and the Mishnah), and *Mysticisme et sociologie*. Appointed to Valence, he became further engaged politically, commenting on the writings of socialist Jules Blanc. Bastide authored a large study on demographics, family life, and social and religious practices among local Armenians, *Les Arméniens de Valence*, which appeared in the *Revue Internationale de Sociologie*. Between 1928 and 1937, Bastide produced just short of one hundred publications, including two books, *Les problèmes de la vie mystique* in 1931 and *Éléments de sociologie religieuse* in 1935. A focus on mysticism linked studies of literature, religion, and sociology.

This book consists of thirteen chapters. After definitional questions, Bastide takes up aspects of religious life (magic, social elements, representational elements, prohibitions, morality, and ritual, termed the "driving elements"), conditions (geographical and social), relations of religious systems to other systems, and the history, origin, and evolution of religion.

Religion, for Bastide, is special within sociology; it cannot be reduced to ordinary social elements. Individual elements are important, too, contra Durkheim. Also, unlike Durkheim, Bastide will not reduce religion to an elementary form but views it in "all its shapes, not only in its primitive form." That will involve ethnography, history, mythology, and contemporary religious phenomena. The comparative method is paramount but with more discipline than is often used, and it is informed by (though not following) Bergson's notion of intuition—apprehending varied religious experiences through introspection and empathy.

Magic's essence, argues Bastide, is to act on and through forces, rather than on and through beings. Magic differs from religion in that it is instrumental, an "operative mechanism." Hence, while magic may involve fasting, virtue, and chastity, these are not moral virtues (as in religion) but mystical properties: "They prevent the loss of magical powers and increase mental concentration, the creator of miracles."

"Representations" are used in Durkheim's sense, to refer to modes of thinking or concepts. Bastide treats such concepts as the soul, spirit, and myth. Some myths are related to ritual. The myth of the suffering, dying god, for example that of Osiris, is related to a sacrificial rite. Other myths, such as that of Orpheus, are not enacted by such rites. Myths can become rites, for example, among the Huichols, where "the pattern of a myth is that of a prayer." Dogmas codify beliefs in the "universal religions, such as Christianity, Buddhism, and Islam," yet such religions retain mythology as nascent dogmas. Dogmas cannot be explained entirely by sociology (à la Durkheim); they are also "the result of deepened spiritual life, which is interior work."

While Bastide's discussion of dogmas and myths is suggestive, even more so is his discussion of relations between taboos and morality. Taboos say no and hence resemble Kant's moral duties, which prohibit or command unconditionally. According to Bastide, "Moral action is necessary in itself and unrelated to any other end. It is an objective necessity." Yet Bastide argues that morality goes beyond taboos through reasoned justification, explaining "Thus morals progressed by eliminating taboos just as medicine progressed by eliminating the idea of possession." He compares sin in Islam and Christianity to taboo: sin is disobeying a divinity, taboo is an infraction that sets sacred powers or demons into action; if taboo is violated, intent is irrelevant. Morality in the major ethical religions, such as Buddhism and Christianity, can lead to a new degree of freedom in action, beyond rigid priestly ethics to "the 'open morality' of the prophet and the inspired." (Here Bastide refers to Bergson.)

Rituals entail, argues Bastide, purification, for example, transferring evil to an object or animal that is then destroyed. This includes revelation of fault: admit the sin, and its influence is stemmed. Rituals also entail divination, for example, foretelling from the flight of a bird or through visionaries and listening to divine voices. Ritual sacrifice is common among humans of all varieties; it survives in Catholicism, in the absorption of God by the community through the priest offering bread and wine, and is paralleled in Australian Intichiuma, when the clan consumes its totem (this from Robertson Smith, extended from his analysis of Arabs sacrificing their camel in the fourth century A.D.). Ritual creates community. Bastide states: "Athenian patriotism became self-conscious during the Pan-Athenian festival. The Last Supper established Catholicism and laid the foundations of Christian internationalism." Initiation ritual introduces the young person into both sexual and social life, a form now exemplified in universities and in military and secret societies that feature secret revelation and "an extension beyond national borders." Note the evocation of nationalism and transnationalism! Prayer, Bastide says, is an "oral ritual," suggested by Mauss in reference to Luther's comments on the Lord's Prayer and those of High German catechists in the eighth and ninth centuries.

What about external conditions of religion? Discussing organization, Bastide echoes or forecasts distinctions between church and sect, tradition and charisma. Religious systems, he suggests, are analogous to biological systems. Geography, he warns, can be linked to religion only indirectly, since humans have modified the environment. He acknowledges links between ceremony and season, but thinks the intervening factor—communal gathering—is crucial. He selects wine production as an example of economics that follows religion rather than geography. Renowned in Egypt and at Carthage, wine was tabooed by Islam yet favored in Christian Communion, and thus is now prominent in temperate climates. Concerning social conditions, he cites Fustel de Coulanges's classic *Cité antique* (Ancient city), showing how religion as ancestor worship shaped family life. He explains the difference between New Englanders and Virginia plantation owners "from the fact that the former lived in large cities, where the pressure of public opinion maintained traditions in their greatest purity, whereas the latter were dispersed, which led to a relaxing of social ties and a weakening of religious constraints." Bastide also cites a similar relationship in Switzerland: emigration weakens religious feeling. Yet religion also shapes society.

Seemingly closed religious systems always interpenetrate: "even in war, there is more assimilation than separation." Examples range from Rome to India, and through the influence of the Chinese sky god on French deism in the eighteenth century to Cadaoism in Indochina.

Religion infuses politics. Kings descended from magicians. Dionysian religion bolstered commoners' struggle against aristocracy, and Freemasonry and Bavarian Illuminism prepared the French Revolution. Yet royalty was related to priests, as shown by the king of France curing scrofula and the German emperor restoring the Holy Roman Empire with Rosicrucian myths.

Marxism, Bastide suggests, is right in arguing that material interests are served through religion. So was Nietzsche, as interpreted by Weber, in claiming religion as a compensation fulfilling needs frustrated in life. Yet just as material needs serve religion, religion shapes material life, as Bastide shows by comparing Protestants to Catholics or tracing the domestication of animals.

Tracing origins is tricky, and Bastide reviews many theories, including Durkheim and Tylor, Andrew Lang and Father Wilhelm Schmidt, as well as the newly emerging Malinowski. He concludes by moving to ethnographic and historical studies; rather than starting with the unknown, the supposed dawn of humankind, he will start with the known and move back as far as feasible. Thus, he goes from monotheism to polytheism back to animism, when the earth was truly a mother, as newborns were placed on the earth.

Evolution from origins leads Bastide to Freud's analogies between phylogeny and ontogeny, thence to certain "laws," which seem generally valid if a bit vapid. He rejects an argument (still prominent today) that religion has lost power by losing breadth of involvement in life. Rather, he says, religion has gained depth and purity through freeing itself from abandoning "fields where it has no reason to be." And religion is moving toward "autonomy of the mystical function." This points toward Bastide's teleology and supports his conclusion, which is that sociology can go only so far in explaining religion, then stops short in this realm of "mysterious seeds and promises of unfamiliar flowers."

Granted, this book is of historical interest: it epitomizes an important transitional period. Beyond that, what do we learn about the phenomenon in question, religion? Bastide addresses far more than the "social origins" of religion; this is not an argument, like Durkheim's or that of the Durkheimians, that religion originates in society. In fact, it is not a focused argument about any origin or cause of religion, although that question is addressed at some points. Instead, this book is a study of religion itself—its nature, its great thematic patterns, its variations, commonalities, origins, and evolution. Although it is short, the work's scope is wide. It encompasses the large theories of an earlier epoch, theories that, like the dinosaurs, have become extinct, replaced by smaller creatures—field studies of a single group or textual studies from a single perspective such as structuralism or feminism. Bastide draws on the vast theories of Frazer, Tylor, Durkheim, and others, but he is not constrained by their particular arguments, and he appears to be equipped by a wide knowledge of classical as well as ethnographic sources in a way few of us match today. From him, then, we learn, or relearn, if we have forgotten, the deep fundamentals of religious life as expressed in history, prehistory, and around the world.

What are these fundamentals? Why are they relevant today? Let us attempt an application. Take as an example the immensely popular quasi-mythological writings of J. R. R. Tolkien, surfacing, as I write, in a celebrated film *The Lord of the Rings*. What are the themes of this epic? The ring was forged by the quintessence of evil, the ruler of Mordor, and the quest of the forces of good is to return this ring to its source and destroy it there. The opposing motive of the evil forces is to repossess the ring and thus regain power and control existence with evil. The story is told from the standpoint of the good, led by an unlikely hero, a small boy from a group of small people, the hobbits, who inhabit a small community, the Shire. The boy, Frodo, receives the ring from his uncle, Bilbo Baggins, who, now more than one hundred years old, disappears from the Shire to go to the land of the elves in order to write a book about his life and history. Frodo, accompanied by the faithful Sam, sets out on a journey. Along the way he picks up a pair of Hobbit roustabouts, a dwarf, and two human warriors, Aragorn and Boromir. Frodo is wounded, healed by the elves, attacked by monster Orcs and nightmarish evil as he plods on toward Mordor, weighed down by the ring and the mission of delivering and destroying it.

The themes of this epic include many fundamental to religious life: ritual; the quest as a rite of passage through life; the passing of energy from old to young; death and rebirth; mentoring by the old; trials, horrors, healing; and sacrifice. Magic appears in wizards who evoke great forces of good or of evil, by words, spells, and a sheer will that smashes material things and controls physical processes. Spirituality, the unseen, is not identified as a God or a Devil but rather a "force" or forces that manifest themselves in creatures and events. Physicality refers to the shire, the goodly land, versus Mordor, the barren, murdered land, and the sites between them (elvish forests, dwarfish caves, and oozing marshes where reside creatures such as Gollum) and bodies: young, aging, killed, renewed.

What would Bastide make of such themes? They are evoked, described phenomenologically, analyzed comparatively by him. Thus, he treats ritual, mythology, magic, and spirituality as phenomena common to human experience. He summarizes the patterns of each: ritual as it follows the life cycle, as it fortifies community, as it sustains governance; mythology, as narrated epics, as fantasy fiction; magic, as practiced and as conceptualized in such terms as "sympathetic" and "contagious" and manifesting forces of good and demonic; and spirituality, as a force in human life that, contrary to Durkheim, transcends social definitions and is expressed in mysticism and pervasive currents that animate all. One would have no difficulty finding in Bastide themes resonant in works such as Tolkien or many others that line long shelves of books, videos, and electronic games that occupy imaginations today. On the other hand, while these universal themes are in Bastide, they are inadequately treated, one might argue, by most of our more specialized anthropological studies today. We anthropologists were so keen to critique and dismiss "armchair" scholarship of the era of Bastide that we have lost the scope of scholarship that he and others mobilized to address the large patterns of human religious life.

What would Bastide miss? Although he notes, in passing, differentiations of class and gender, not to mention, by implication, at least, race, he is not so concerned with such issues of "difference" and inequality as are many contemporary thinkers. His theories would not lead one to notice, for example, seeming prejudices in Tolkien. In *Lord of the Rings*, it is men or masculine creatures and forces that motivate the quest and struggle, while women, though present and sometimes powerful, are healers, helpmates, and temptresses. On the other hand, Tolkien's philosophy is not elitist. His hero is a small, young person, not wealthy—a sturdy semirural, modest, unexpectedly resourceful and solidly virtuous ordinary character—salt of the earth. It is true he is not without means; he is the inheritor of a ring and presumably property in the shire, yet he does not crave power and status; it is the nobility and aristocracy who, though heroic and heroinic, also succumb to the lure of power and sometimes are corrupted. And although the spectrum of creatures is vast—from Orcs and elves to dwarves and humans—they are Caucasian, not Asian or African, framed within a mythology that is northern European; diversity is limited.

Noticing such omissions (in Bastide, paralleled by Tolkien), one would also note "sins of commission" that are also a focus of contemporary commentary: Bastide is "colonialist." Similar to others of his time, he refers on occasion to primitives or "inferior" peoples—at least this is the way the translation renders his French, presumably "inférieur," which means "lower." His viewpoint is that of the enlightened European looking out at and sometimes down on the rest of the world. One does not find, in this colonial period, for example, Bastide's juxtaposition of Durkheim and Bergson in dialogue with an authoritative postcolonial new nation philosopher on the same subject; see the excellent work by Djuretna A. Imam Muhni, *Moral dan Religi: Menurut Emile Durkheim dan Henri Bergson* (Morals and religion: Concerning Emile Durkheim and Henri Bergson), published by Penerbit Kansius, Yogyakarta, Indonesia, in 1994. Bastide observes the non-European world; he is not in intellectual dialogue with it—an "orientalist" stance still pervasive. Still, in practice, he is fairly inclusive and evenhanded. He is attentive to both "primitive" and "civilized" religious practice (even today, it is difficult to find a term for these which is readily known and not pejorative); as noted, he describes Catholic Christian Communion or other ritual practices and beliefs together with rituals among "primitives" that included eating sacred totems—a comparison familiar to other writers of the day, including Freud and Robertson Smith, as he notes. When we dismiss Bastide or others for their colonialism, we should recognize that their comparative framework was used to critique claims of special privilege by missionaries and colonial officials by implying that all religious practice, indeed, culture in general, was panhuman in basics.

In sum, Bastide brings not only a historically interesting period piece, but revives and extends our thinking about religion in a comparative panhuman framework. Comparative method is getting a new look today, stimulated by attention to globalism, which pushes us past localized studies. So is the anthropology of religion, which, after a period of submergence within cultural studies, is being energized, for example, by a new section on the anthropology of religion within the American Anthropological Association. Beyond disciplinary and academic boundaries, predictions of secularism have been replaced by awareness of threatening religious forces in the world, new cults, fundamentalism. In this context, Bastide serves as a useful revisiting of a broader perspective on religious life, a revisiting that may in part revitalize.

Preface

At the present time, both in France and abroad, the study of religious phenomena is of prime importance in the social sciences. Unfortunately, too many researchers of unequal learning have tried to write on this subject and have combined a number of rash and arbitrary hypotheses with duly established facts. Our theory is that a positive sociology of religion can have a valid foundation only if careful distinctions are made between the following:

> Facts resulting from rigorous examination of the evidence;
>
> Hypotheses and explanatory theories, which have a legitimate place in the sociology of religion as in all other sciences of observation, as long as they remain scientific;
>
> Theories that fly too far from the facts and in which metaphysics pierces through pseudopositivistic language. As interesting as these theories may be, they cannot claim to provide accurate interpretations of reality.

In this work, I have tried to observe these distinctions carefully. First I define the sociology of religion and delimit the sphere of the sacred. Then I proceed with an analytic study of the principal social features of religious life: shared representations, taboos, rituals, and religions. We go on to the synthetic study of religious systems, which are examined globally, both in themselves and in their relation to all of social life. A rapid examination of the major theories on the origin and evolution of religion ends this work.

R. B., 1935

The Object, Limits, and Method of the Sociology of Religion

Sociology is the study of societies. Thus, at first sight it seems that two sociologies of religion could be possible, depending on whether one considers *religion* to mean the society of men with gods or only the society of men sharing the same dogmas and participating in the same rituals.

The former view was that of Guyau in *L'Irréligion de l'avenir* (1902), but its most important endorsement comes from de la Grasserie, for whom every religion unites the living with the dead and the faithful with the gods in a vast society, the study of which belongs to cosmology.

We will not investigate this view to any great degree. To begin with, it is based on a dubious etymology since it traces *religio* from *religare*, to unite, whereas this word is more usually shown to derive from *religere*, to worship with fear and respect. But let us assume etymology is not important. What is more serious is that this view takes gods to be objective realities, as beings, in de la Grasserie's words. Thus cosmology studies the relations such beings have with each other: relations of friendship (Isis and Osiris, etc.) or hate (the war between the gods and the giants, etc.). Yet this definition reduces cosmology to pure mythology, or, if one prefers to consider not the relations between the gods but those between the gods and us, it implies that there is some hidden reality behind mythical appearances, that there is a mysterious relation between us as persons and something that has no name. While it is true that the view that people have of their relation to the gods, which varies depending on beliefs, is a legitimate subject for study, it in no way expresses objectively observable social relations. Thus what must be studied is not the society of men with the gods, but the ideas people have about such a society. However, here we move on to the other view of the sociology of religion: that which studies groupings based on shared beliefs and practices. This is the sociology of religion to which the vast majority of sociologists subscribe.

Certainly, direct religious feeling is specifically human before it is social. However, it develops only when it is shared by believers. Everything mystical becomes incarnate in a church. The church is a community and, as such, it is subject to the laws of all communities, the very ones that sociology tries to identify by observing data. But it is a community limited to the sphere of the sacred, and, under such conditions, the laws to which it is subject naturally take on a special nature. Thus the need for a special science to formulate them and for a sociology of religion within sociology. But can such a sociology be limited to the comparative study of religions?

The sociologists of the *Année sociologique* school have an unfortunate tendency to virtually eliminate individual facts. Durkheim certainly recognizes that today believers can rebel against traditions and that some may construct, in their secret hearts, new lifestyles, but he immediately adds that such individual beliefs amount to little when compared with those that are shared. Religion is by nature a social fact.

It is a social fact, first, owing to its very uniformity: "There is no personal religion that is entirely original; the most independent thinker lives on traditional ideas."[1]

Next, it is a social fact because religious phenomena, such as myths and rituals, somehow exist independently of individuals. They have a sui generis reality. The same action, for example a sacrifice, may have been justified in different ways over time, but the structure of the ceremony remains unchanged over generations.

Finally, it is a social fact because of its coercive power: religious beliefs are imposed from outside on the submissive, obedient believer. They are sanctioned, sometimes legally (excommunication) but always morally, even in the most individualistic societies, such as the Anglo-Saxon countries.

This is not the time to criticize a thesis that confuses the religious with the collective. We will see the importance of individual factors throughout these pages. Of Durkheim's ideas, all we need to remember at present is that the communal penetrates deeply into the religious. In the sociology of religion we must thus make room, next to the study of the formation and development of religions, for that of collective ideas and actions. Thus we will finally define the object of our science by saying that it includes religious societies, myths, dogmas, and rituals.

What is the place of the sociology of religion, so defined, within sociology as a whole? It probably does not cover the entire field, but it is a fundamental part of it, from the beginning.

Sociology dates from Comte. According to the Law of the Three Stages, to which he of course accorded prime importance, the new science is for the founder of positivism largely a history of the human mind. Essentially religious thought is the first stage in the intellectual development of humanity, as it is in the intellectual development of the individual. Logical thought emerged from religious beliefs gradually. In a way, Comte foretold the framework in which the sociology of religion was to develop in France. By showing the "theological" nature of primitive mentality, he anticipated the work of Lévy-Bruhl, just as by making sociology the history of the human mind, he prefigured the last works of Durkheim.

In those of his works we will be using, Lévy-Bruhl attempted to describe the way primitives think. Savages indeed have the same sense organs we have. They perceive natural phenomena in the same way as the civilized, but their perceptions are immediately enveloped in complex states of consciousness dominated by feelings with religious tones. The thought of a primitive is above all "mystical." Certainly, it is difficult to know the original state of the human mind. Yet Lévy-Bruhl's books at least warn us of the extreme difficulty we will have in distinguishing the religious thought of primitives from their other systems of thought, and religion from the rest of society. Nevertheless, we cannot wholly endorse Lévy-Bruhl's point of view, for under the pretext that all savage activity, be it military, economic, or familial, has a "mystical" nature, we would risk incorporating virtually all of ethnography into the sociology of religion.

However, Durkheim's distinction between the sacred and the profane in *The Elementary Forms of the Religious Life* (1915) will help us to delimit the field to which we confine ourselves in this book: the sociology of religion. In order to avoid crossing over the limits we have set, we will adopt the head of the French school of sociology's justified concern with defining the religious fact in its greatest purity. We will not follow him right to the end, however. He focused essentially on the study of primitive religions and tried to identify the religious with the communal and to extract from ethnographical research not only the various natures and laws of the thought of religious groups, but also the internal laws of the development of the human mind as it generates logic and science from notions such as mana. In short, he was inclined to transform the study of the sociology of religion into a theory of knowledge.

Our goal will be both more modest and more far-reaching: more modest because we will restrict ourselves to examining collective religious facts and will thus leave aside all that touches on the problem of knowledge; more far-reaching because we will consider religious life in all its shapes, not only in its primitive form.

Where shall we look for our raw material? First, of course, to the comparative history of religion, whether it examines the data without taking sides or does so from the point of view of a specific religion (Egyptian religion, for example, in the case of Foucart). Next we will look to

ethnography, which will enable us to extend our compar-
isons by opening our research to the vast field of noncivilized peoples. We will also look to mythology, since, as
we have said, myths are at least partially social facts. We
must also not neglect current religious phenomena as they
occur in our Western societies, for "the present is just as
revealing of the past as the past is of the present. More
advanced social knowledge and clearer ideas make possible
a better grasp of the true nature of functions that are very
obscure in their primitive forms" (Belot). This approach
is consistent with the recommendation that statistics be
used to show how religious data evolve in accordance with
demographic data, such as urban density, mixtures of races,
and emigration. However, used in their raw form, statistics
would lead us into error. We must interpret them through
our own experience of religious life, and this leads us to a
serious methodological problem.

When we use our own experience, do we not risk dis-
torting our vision of religious realities by introducing
"prenotions" between them and us? This was Durkheim's
view, and he recommended that social facts always be considered as objects, which amounts to completely condemning introspection. "No one studying religion," he said,
"should ever take the least account of his own experience."
This argument does not appear decisive to Pinard de la
Boulaye who, while recognizing that the believer "puts
everything on the line" in the religious domain, thinks that
for the nonbeliever "the stakes are opposite, but equal."
Renan, Darmesteter, and Richard believe, on the contrary,
that "if the first condition for being able to speak of art or

poetry with any discernment is to have felt poetry and art oneself, the first condition required of he who wishes to understand the believer and societies of believers is to have, at some point in his life and at least through affection and sentiment, shared a belief."

Personally, we think that intuitive sympathy should not be lacking in the sociologist. However, introspection should remain a secondary process, a sort of safety net, which prevents us from adopting arbitrary hypotheses. Here the comparative method is, as in all other branches of sociology, the essential one.

Yet certain precautions must be taken when it is employed:

1. We must avoid borrowing from all peoples and all times to accumulate similar details (despite the fact that this is a method honored by English anthropologists and sometimes by those in our own country). In science it is not useful to multiply examples beyond a certain point: a single good observation can sometimes shed light on an extremely general law. Moreover, the procedure of massive accumulation targets only identification. Differentiation is also important, if not more so. As Hubert and Mauss say, "[These anthropologists] go straight to the similarities, and everywhere they look, they seek only what is human and shared: in short, banal. In contrast, our method is to focus on the differences characteristic of specific settings. It is through such characteristics that we hope to glimpse laws." Indeed, when the goal is to reveal similarities, care must be taken to compare only things that

are comparable and not to mix (unless there are special reasons to do so) data on peoples as savage as the Negritos with that on peoples as cultivated as the Chinese.

2. The analytic approach is the only one possible for researchers. First, monographs on a myth or rite must undergo comparative study. However, this process is dangerous if used exclusively. Even if a religion is rich in foreign elements, it nonetheless forms a whole. Thus, if one singles out an element, such as an idea or a ceremony, from the system of which it is a part in order to study it in isolation, there is a risk of misinterpretation, since it is the whole that explains the part and not the parts that make sense of the whole.

3. Finally, the observation of a similarity tells us nothing, in itself, about its value or meaning. Interpretation is always required. Here there are three possibilities:

Such similarities could be owing to direct or indirect transmission between peoples.

They could also result from the identity of the human mind, which reacts similarly in like circumstances.

Finally, they could be caused by the influence of similar external environments.

One school, that of cultural history, is more in agreement with the first hypothesis. Another, that of English ethnologists, favors the second. Two others, the French sociological school and the American "convergence" school, endorse the latter. Those two schools hold that ideological analogies (dogmas, myths, etc.) result from analogies between social structures or physical organization. Such diversity in points of view thus requires caution.

It is in this spirit and with this method that we will now begin the study of the sociology of religion.

Part I. The Sphere of the Sacred

CHAPTER 1

Definition of Religion

There are innumerable definitions of religion, and every philosopher has one to suggest. In order to find a path through this chaos, we will study the introspective, intuitive, and objective definitions separately.

When we wonder about religion's essence and try to forget the dogmas and rituals of our own religion so as to go further and beyond to rediscover the original feeling, then we define religion as, for example, the impression we have of swimming in a sea of mystery (Spencer); the feeling either of the infinite (Max Müller) or our dependency on a being greater than us (Schleiermacher); or, sometimes, the instinct that spurs us toward happiness (Feuerbach).

Such definitions, of which we could easily give many more examples, all have the defect of being too individual and therefore not covering the whole generality of the religious fact. They can be used as a foundation for a philosophy of which we could feel the fervor or pathos, but not as one for a science. Indeed, they seem to be recent ideas, for example, the entirely modern distinction between the natural and the supernatural, or the notions conveyed by our Christian education (the feeling of the infinite, etc.), for Christianity has formed the very hearts of those who rebel against it.

The introspective method, as it is usually practiced, thus cannot provide a valid definition of religion. However, Bergson has recently changed this method to such an extent that it is perhaps now better able to apprehend the subject of its research. This new form of introspection has been given the special name of *intuition*. If we can, through a heroic effort, tear ourselves away from the influence of the external environment and forget for a minute the intellectual and emotional habits society has deposited in us, then we may reach through the sedimentary layers to the bedrock, the very essence of religious life.

If acquired habits could be inherited, then the unending acquisitions of humanity would have covered that primary foundation by now. They would have changed it so much that there would be a veritable abyss between the people of today and those of the past. Thus intuition would be able to attain only the present forms of religious feeling. However, the heredity of acquired habits has not been proved: "The natural is today the same as it always was." And we can go beyond the social to reach it. While it is true that the effort required is of a rare degree, exceptional circumstances can greatly facilitate this quest: "A sudden surprise paralyzes superficial activities or the light in which they take place goes out for an instant: immediately the natural reappears, like an eternal star in the night."

The great merit of such a method would be that it could penetrate through the social and reach the biological. More precisely, since the biological cannot be reached through introspection, it would be able to access the point where biology changes into an object of consciousness. Thus intuition would have a chance of discovering the true essence of religion.

Navigating by such soundings, Bergson manages to define what he calls *static religion* as "a defensive reaction of nature against what might be depressing for the individual, and dissolvent for the society, in the exercise of intelligence" (Bergson 1935, 194 [1932, 219]).

Unfortunately, this new definition must be left aside. Methodologically, it is linked to a theory of intuition that is not universally accepted, and theoretically, it is based on the thesis of the élan vital, which, in spite of its goal of "embracing experience" as closely as possible, remains for many a metaphysical idea that is not scientifically verifiable.

We are thus led to the comparative method. We must compare ancient and modern, primitive and civilized, and living and dead religions to identify and focus on only the elements they share.

This method generally results in definitions like that of Frazer, who considers religion to begin with the appearance of the notion of gods, or at least of individual spirits, souls of the dead or genies of nature, modeled on men and women. Primitive rituals, which are based on the idea of impersonal, mystical forces, would have their origin in pure magic and would not be specifically religious at all.

However, Durkheim objects that there are, even among civilized peoples, major religions without gods or spirits. Buddha is not a god because "he has no control over the progression of human events"; he is dissolved in nirvana and can be considered only as the "wisest of men." His disciples do not seek salvation through prayer or faith. They rely on themselves alone to gain it. Jainism is also an atheist religion. As for Brahmanism, at one point in its development did it not eliminate the ancient Vedic gods and replace them with an abstract, thus impersonal, principle, the Brahma?

Moreover, even in religions that include gods we find a number of rituals that overflow with animism: "The Bible orders women to live in isolation for a specific period each month . . . , it prohibits the yoking of the donkey and the horse together, the wearing of clothing in which hemp is mixed with linen." For the Aryans, the effectiveness of sacrifice is not caused by the gods to which it is addressed: sacrifice is "all-powerful in itself." Thus religions cannot be defined by the idea of gods or spirits.

The only element that is really shared by all is a much wider notion, which Durkheim claims is the sacred:

> All known religious beliefs . . . presuppose a classification of all the things, real and ideal, of which men think, into two classes or opposed groups, generally designated by two distinct terms which are translated well enough by the words *profane* and *sacred (profane, sacré)* . . . by sacred things one must not understand simply those personal beings which are called gods or spirits; a rock, a tree, a spring, a pebble, a piece of wood, a house, in a word, anything can be sacred. A rite can have this character; . . . words, expressions and formulae. (Durkheim 1915, 37 [1912, 50–51])

Moreover this distinction is not simply a matter of degree. It is an opposition between natures. Between the two domains there is absolute heterogeneity.

Yet this distinction must be made even stronger. The profane is more than just the negation of the sacred. It cannot be defined simply as everything that is not involved in what is religious. As Hertz has shown in his monograph on the preeminence of the right hand, the profane, owing to its separation from the sacred, becomes an antagonistic element that is dangerous for the sacred and alters, corrupts, and reduces the strength of mystical forces. For example, because women are excluded from religious ceremonies, they come to be thought of as witches and casters of spells. Since the right hand is clean, the left hand, which is at first without any influence of its own, becomes harmful. Thus the profane inclines toward the impure, to form, through its opposition to the sacred, the negative pole of the spiritual world. The distinction between the magical and the religious is therefore understandable. It would be only a secondary transformation of the primitive distinction between the profane and the sacred. Except that magic, like religion, has its myths and rites. Therefore, Durkheim's definition of the religious by the sacred could be too broad, whereas Frazer's initially appears too narrow.

Thus we must reexamine the problem of the relations between religion and magic. This will be the subject of the next chapter.

CHAPTER 2

Magic

As in the case of religion, magic is relatively difficult to define. First, when one religion triumphs over another, as when Christianity supplanted paganism, the victorious customarily call the rituals of the vanquished magical, despite the fact that defeat does not alter the initial forms of the rituals. Magical practices also vary from country to country: Egyptians used them to obtain prosperity, whereas Chaldeans employed them as protection from lurking evil. Above all, in the superstitions of many peoples it is possible to discern several successive layers and stratifications.

All the various forms of magic can be boiled down to two sorts of practices: those that call on the mediation of spirits and those that, duly regulated, act directly on nature.

Christian magic is indirect magic. Warlocks and witches have made a pact with Satan. They fly on grotesque brooms to the midnight Sabbath, where a backward mass is celebrated on a barren hill. However, Christian magic is not the only one based on the existence of supernatural spirits: the same was true of the Greco-Roman magic that preceded it, which invoked demons, called the spirits of the dead up from the depths of the earth, made the moon come down from the sky, and summoned the intervention of Hecate and Selene. This bespeaks the strong influence of eastern magic, in which demonology knows no bounds. India, finally, is also not ignorant of evil spirits, but its demonology is no longer so straightforward. "Evil (pâpman) is sometimes a neutral object, sometimes a harmful being" (Oldenberg). In their secret, and often malefic, ceremonies, primitives also summon either the souls of the dead, such as the Melanesian *tindalos*, or spirits similar to our demons, such as the Aruntas' Iruntarinia.

However, it should be noted that in demonic magic impersonal powers come into play. A spirit can be evoked by a magician, but it does not come entirely of its own will. It yields to the dominating power of the words or actions. Sometimes the influence of a rite or a magical liturgy even triumphs over the desperate efforts of an evil spirit, for example, exorcism may chase one away, despite much gnashing of teeth. Thus Tylor's animist thesis, which tries to derive magic from belief in spirits, is unsatisfactory: demonology cannot explain everything. Moreover, the demons evoked by the appropriate rites do not generally have the well-defined personality of the Christian devil. Most often their individuality is vague at best. Their names are less those of persons than they are of species, and so cover a host of anonymous beings.

Let us go further. Sometimes we can discover the genesis of demonic magic. In Islam there is a whole series of rituals in which it seems that the invoker creates the spirit that will be used, since the rite is named and thus tends to become a person, or that there are the forces against which the magician fights, which become individualized, as in the case of illnesses. In contrast, we can observe the magical deindividualization of gods. Greco-Roman magic used the gods of religion, such as Selene, Hecate, and Zeus, but it removed from them everything that made them unique, even to the point of replacing them by letters (X = Osiris, Z = Apis, etc.). In other words, the essence of the magical ceremony is to act on and by forces, rather than on and by beings.

Demonic magic thus appears to be preceded by another simpler form known as natural magic, which does not summon the strength of spirits but is based on impersonal principles regulating the course of nature:

> first, that like produces like; ... second, that things which have once been in contact with each other continue to act on each other at a distance after the physical contact has been severed. The former principle may be called the Law of Similarity, the latter the Law of Contact or Contagion. From the first of these principles, namely the Law of Similarity, the magician infers that he can produce any effect he desires merely by imitating it: from the second he infers that whatever he does to a material object will affect equally the person with whom the object was once in contact, whether it formed part of his body or not. Charms based on the Law of Similarity may be called Homeopathic or Imitative Magic. Charms based on the Law of Contact or Contagion may be called Contagious Magic. (Frazer 1957, 14)

Contagious magic is based on the idea that objects that were united, even if only once, remain forever linked by a sort of secret solidarity. If a man's tooth falls to the ground and is swallowed by a dog, the man's other teeth will become as hard as those of the dog. If instead ants walk on the tooth, its former owner will suffer a toothache. Imitative magic, such as erected stones used in sexual or fertility ceremonies and totemic dances that copy the actions and appearance of a totemic animal, is intended to ensure that what it represents multiplies. The similar is always evoked by the similar and, in the case of medical superstitions, ensures the patient's recovery. Moreover, the law of similarity has its counterpart in the law of opposites: "In the atharvanic ritual, rain is made to end by summoning the sun using arka wood" (Hubert and Mauss).

Of course, the savage does not formulate these two laws with the precision and exactitude we give them. The primitive does not speculate: "[H]e never analyses the mental processes on which his practice is based, never reflects on the abstract principles involved in his actions.... he reasons just as he digests his food in complete ignorance of the intellectual and physiological processes which are essential to the one operation and to the other" (Frazer 1957, 15).

It is no less true that, if this analysis is sound, all natural magic rests on rational principles. This is why many anthropologists have made magic the result of "intellectual work," humanity's initial attempt to explain natural phenomena (King). Frazer saw it more often as the result in the savage's thought of spontaneous association of ideas: "If my analysis of the magician's logic is correct, its two great principles turn out to be merely two different misapplications of the association of ideas. Homeopathic magic is founded on the association of ideas by similarity; contagious magic is founded on the association of ideas by contiguity" (Frazer 1957, 15).

Despite Frazer's great authority, we do not think it is possible to reduce all of magic to the operation, even the defective operation, of the laws of thought. That formulas of association

> can serve to classify magical processes there is no doubt. But it in no wise follows that magical operations are derived from them. If primitive intelligence had begun by conceiving principles it would very soon have recapitulated before the evidence of experience, which would have proved them erroneous. But here again it merely translates into a conception of what was suggested by an instinct. To put it more clearly, there is a logic of the body, an extension of desire, which comes into play long before intelligence has found a conceptual form for it. (Bergson 1935, 156 [1932, 17])

We will come back to the logic of desire at work in magic. However we can make a new objection to the "intellectualist" theory. If we look closely at how the laws of contiguity and similarity behave in magic, we soon see that they cannot be the simple, inevitable product of the association of ideas. For, between the image and the object of imitative magic, there is in the end only a vague, completely conventional, resemblance. In one bewitchment rite, the adversary is killed by piercing a wax statuette with a pin, but the rough statuette has no need to resemble, even in the least, the person to be killed. It is sufficient to think that the piece of wax represents the person. Physical representation can even be left out. The statuette can be replaced by the heart of an animal or an onion. What is important is that something be pierced. This explains why the same object may be used in completely different ceremonies. The head of a poppy, for example, can symbolize rain, thunder, the sun, fever, or a child to be born, depending on the case. In other words, in magic there is considerable interpretation, and thus much more is involved than the simple products of the laws of association.

Where should we look for the true sources of magic? Perhaps we will find them by beginning with the fact, which Frazer barely notices, that in addition to magical actions there is a magic of speech. Perhaps by examining this we will find an explanation of the genesis of magic:

> Incantation, curse, and blessing appear to be the three main forms . . . that this third form of magic takes. By saying to an arrow: "Go straight and kill," the arrow is aided in its deadly task. Among North American Indians, it is a general practice to project one's thoughts and will at a distance. A. Fletcher says, "When there is a race a man can direct his thoughts and will onto one of the competitors with the idea that such an action, such a projection of one's spirit, will help his friend to win." In this case, it seems the strength of the will itself accomplishes the magical action, but most often certain words are used to carry the will or strength of one individual into another. According to Kohl, "All happy or sad emotions turn into a magical song in the mouth of an Indian. If you ask him to sing a hymn to nature or a simple hunting verse, he never gives you anything but a sort of incantation he says can be used to make birds come out of the sky and foxes out of their dens." (Allier)

This third form of magic thus conveys the effectiveness of the desire. If we can prove that it is the most primitive, we will have sufficient proof that magic has its roots in emotions and not in defective use of the intellect.

When the warriors are out hunting or fighting, the elders and women left behind in the village think only about the victory of the men who are gone. They cannot help but exteriorize this intense emotion, and if the warriors come back victorious it appears to all that the intensity of their desire has become reality. A savage who shoots an arrow puts his whole soul into it. He speaks to it in his mind and tells it to "go straight to the target." Since he also spends that time aiming so as not to miss, he imagines that his success is due to his wish.

Imitative magic, of which we said a few words earlier, is only the extension of such incantative magic. A man who desires does not just talk. He sketches out the movements he would like to see. Bergson imagines,

> for instance, a "primitive" man who wants to kill his enemy: that enemy, however, is far away; it is impossible to get at him. No matter! Our man is in a rage; he goes through the motions of pouncing on the absent man. Once started he goes on to the bitter end; he squeezes his fingers round the neck of the victim he thinks he has hold of or wants to have hold of, and throttles him. But he knows very well that the result is not complete. He has done everything that he himself could do: he demands that things should do the rest. (Bergson 1935, 156 [1932, 176])

Faith in the effectiveness of the rite is thus but the extension of faith in the effectiveness of the word: "Imitation has its roots in action, not in association" (Delacroix).

Sympathetic magic has no other explanation, and here emotion again plays a fundamental role. As Allier says, "We must not forget that all that is needed is a fraction of the idea to arouse the emotion linked to the perception of the whole idea. A tiger's claw awakens the memory of the whole tiger and of what one feels before it." The lover evokes the memory of his mistress by regarding a ribbon or a dried flower. From this, we can see how a primitive possessing an object that used to belong to his lover or his enemy can imagine that he has that person at his mercy through the object. The object is already the entire person.

We find desires and emotional ideas at work at the origin of magic everywhere. Civilized people themselves confirm this thesis indirectly, for every time reasoning ceases and emotion surges forth like an irresistible wave, magic is immediately reborn. For example, a gambler in Monaco may allow himself to be dominated by his anxiety, and, whether he wins or loses, he observes the objects around him and the circumstances in which he finds himself. He does not attribute his good or bad luck to skill or chance. He believes it is certain objects and special circumstances that mysteriously influenced the game. He imagines a mystical causality. Is this not the threshold of magic?

Is this thesis wholly satisfactory? Is psychology alone sufficient to explain the totality of magical phenomena, or does it offer only the beginnings of an explanation?

An important aspect of magic has been left aside: its conventional, traditional nature. First, in imitative magic it should be noted that all the features of a symbol are not transmitted to the symbolized. Only one is retained: from clay, its pliability; from money, its shine. This is an extremely artificial abstraction which is transmitted from generation to generation. Among other things, the number of symbols used within a social group is very limited. The magic of knots is used for a thousand things: to snuff out love, calm the wind, stop evil, cure illness, and so on. The individual is thus not free to choose the objects he will use to achieve his desire. He must submit himself to the omnipotence of tradition.

Magic is indeed, in final analysis, the externalization of desire, but the latter deserves to be called magic only when it becomes a social phenomenon. We will come to an analogous conclusion as we go from sorcery to the sorcerer.

If the psychological thesis alone could explain magic, then we could all be magicians whenever we wanted. However, a magical rite is generally performed by a specialist, such as a sorcerer. What is the source of this differentiation? What creates a sorcerer? After having studied the intellectualist and emotional theories of magic, we will look at one last theory, the metaphysical theory. According to it, we have powers of which we are unaware. Perhaps the sorcerers have learned to harness them? Who knows whether science, as it has developed, has not made our intelligence more superficial and shallow and thus unable to apprehend the mysterious energies that the less refined heart of the savage perceives?

Many missionaries and explorers have been struck by the ability of sorcerers to divine. Apparently, Trilles learned from one of them that his father had died before he received the news from more usual sources. Another announced to Vaffer that ships would arrive, despite the fact that none were expected. Europeans witnessed a sorcerer raise the beam on which his apprentice was sitting and make it twirl around without touching it, using only the power of his will. Imbert-Gourbeyre claims to have seen natives raise themselves two or three feet in the air and walk on the tips of grasses. "A sorcerer took a container full of water, raised it in his hands, then slowly moved his palms away from the sides of the container, which remained suspended in the air" (Trilles). Through the intermediary of another sorcerer, the same missionary claims to have sent a message by instant thought transmission to an evangelist who was a four-day walk from his location.

If such data were truly authentic, then magic would have an objective, experimental value. It would be the application of suprasensory gifts and abilities that we have unfortunately allowed to gradually atrophy because they are dangerous.

This thesis has already been defended by Lang in *The Making of Religion* (1899) and taken up again by Leroy in *La raison primitive* (1927). However, the documents we possess are too rare, come from people whose critical abilities are not well enough known, and relate data too much in opposition to what we see for us to trust them blindly. Perhaps in the cases reported there was simply the sorcerer's intense power of suggestion over the spectators?

It has also been claimed that magic, far from being the result of miraculous powers, is instead produced by mental illness. Bastian argued this. Without wanting to engage in a discussion beyond our competencies, it can be noted that a magician's training could only exacerbate his excitability. For example, in order to reach the Akhoung, a Fan sorcerer must remain in a ditch for several days, attached to the corpse of a man he has killed, mouth to mouth, body to body, and without eating or drinking. How could he come out of such a trial without visions and ecstatic cries?

Yet even if neurosis were involved, it would not be sufficient to produce a magician. It would only lay the groundwork. The society must also recognize the individual as a magician, and especially, the magician must fashion his neurotic states to the framework preestablished by tradition.

Hubert and Mauss used Australian societies as the point of departure in their study of the origin of magical powers. Such powers are sometimes hereditary: there are families and corporations of sorcerers. For example, one need only be born into the caste of shepherds or blacksmiths to be considered a magician. Most often, those who are to become magicians have revelations, but the spirit that appears to the apprentice sorcerer is not free to act any way it pleases. Even the most minor details of the vision are regulated by the community. For example, in the Sydney tribe, the spirit cuts the sleeper's throat and changes his entrails; in that of Port-Macquarie, it inserts a magical bone into his thigh; among the Arunta, it pierces the future sorcerer with a lance, kills him, carries him off to the depths of a cave, removes his entrails and stuffs him with quartz crystals. Thus the society provides a kind of framework for the dream or hallucination. Moreover, revelation is not sufficient: tradition is added. Whatever the importance of direct contact with the spirits, the magician must also learn the myths and rituals, formulas and movements. In short, a complete oral education is transmitted from generation to generation.

Thus society, or at least the secret society, weighs wholly on the magician to regulate his hallucination and provide him with a ready-made tradition.

Thus we come to the same conclusion as before. If we are to understand the origin of magic, sociology must complete the psychological findings.

We can see from the preceding paragraphs how far we are from those who view magic as an initial version of science. Yet this is a long-standing opinion that sees the origin of chemistry in alchemy, that of astronomy in astrology, that of medicine in the art of potions, and that of arithmetic in theories of the mystical values of numbers. This opinion was that of the first sociologist, Comte, but has taken a new form among modern ethnologists and, of course, is supported by all those who, like Frazer, take an intellectualist approach to magic:

> Wherever sympathetic magic occurs in its unadulterated form, it assumes that in nature one event follows another necessarily and invariably without the intervention of any spiritual or personal agency. Thus its fundamental conception is identical with that of modern science; underlying the whole system is a faith, implicit but real and firm, in the order and uniformity of nature. The magician does not doubt that the same causes will always produce the same effects, that the performance of the proper ceremony, accompanied by the appropriate spell, will inevitably be attended by the desired result, unless, indeed, his incantations should chance to be thwarted and foiled by the more potent charms of another sorcerer.... Thus the analogy between magical and scientific conceptions of the world is close. In both of them the succession of events is assumed to be perfectly regular and certain, being determined by immutable laws, the operation of

which can be foreseen and calculated precisely; the elements of caprice, or chance, and of accident are banished from the course of nature. (Frazer 1957, 63–64)

Thus magic's special gift to science would be universal determinism. Certainly, magic makes poor use of the principles of similarity and contiguity, yet it is not wrong to use them, for science is also the search for hidden resemblances and causal contiguities. Thus magic is "the illegitimate sister" of science.

What seems to give credence to this idea is the fact that magic and science pursue the same goal: human control over nature. To govern the world, magic must necessarily come into contact with it. It is thus led to perform all sorts of experiments and can contain, under a mystical cloak, much positive knowledge. To limit ourselves to a single example, Berthelot was able to show, and document, all the science that was already contained in the tradition of alchemy.

Yet even though a certain amount of accurate knowledge may have slipped into sorcery, it did not result from the principles of magic themselves. It was the work of impartial observations and critical induction that were not introduced into the ancient tradition except after the fact and as if by chance. Moreover, the reason people believe this knowledge is accurate is not because it was discovered using positive processes. It has the same sort of certainty as that attributed to the rest of magic: mystical certainty. This means it is, in Essertier's words, more a "quasi science" than a true science. The proof is that disconfirmation does not lead to progress in magic, whereas it guarantees such progress in science. Did the rainmaker's rite fail? That will not lead the sorcerer to try to modify the laws he used in order to make his technique more appropriate to experience. Instead he will accuse a more powerful sorcerer of having prevented the effect of his charms and will therefore commit himself more deeply to his first mistake.

Thus even when magic seems to come closest to science and contains a certain amount of correct knowledge, magic and science still do not merge. On the contrary, there is a marked opposition between the two.

The primary quality of the scientist is a critical mind, and science is born only on the day when the authority of reason is substituted for that of the elders. Magic, on the contrary, is governed by tradition. The sorcerer is in no way permitted to change what has been transmitted to him from the distant past. If he were to make the slightest modification, the expected effect would not be produced. This is the first difference, one of method.

As we have said, there are laws of magic, but such laws call upon occult powers, and their causality is mystical, not natural. Scientific laws are established only through observations and experiments, and all that cannot be verified is rejected immediately. This is the second difference, one of spirit.

Finally, a sorcerer who wants to discover guilt looks for no clues and evaluates no testimony: he makes the suspect drink poison and waits, confident of its effectiveness. Thus what comes into play in magic is the law of least effort. It is simpler to rely on destiny than to perform a long and often arduous inquiry. The defining quality of a scientist is, on the contrary, perseverance. Courage and energy are often required. Science and magic are indeed opposites and far from similar. This should not surprise us, since the former has a speculative origin while the latter springs from desire and emotion.

As Essertier notes, everything is employed in magical ceremonies to intensify fear and heighten desire. The time: pale dawn, twilight, or most often, fear-inspiring night. The place: eerie graveyard under the white light of the moon, deserted crossroads or moors. The ceremony is conducted with priestly bearing. While a technique is used, it is an entirely emotional technique that has nothing in common with that of Bacon's "dry-eyed" scientist.

Yet there was a time when magic was oriented toward science, with occultism, alchemy, and astrology, or are we being deceived once again? The *magia naturalis* of the Middle Ages did boast of experiments, but the only thing those experiments had in common with our own was the name. Alchemy was not guided by the quest for truth, but by the desire for riches and power. It was always qualitative and neglected measurement. Chemistry was born the day Lavoisier brought scales into the laboratory: "Nothing is less exact than to claim that chemistry was born of alchemy; it was not even born out of its ruins. It succeeded it by assassinating it, like the priest of Nemi."

We could go even further. Not only is magic not science and not only did it not give birth to science, but it was the biggest obstacle to science's appearance:

> Civilized man is a being in whom incipient science,
> implicit in the daily round, has been able to encroach,
> thanks to an ever-active will, on that magic which was
> occupying the rest of the field. Noncivilized man is, on

the contrary, one who, disdaining effort, has allowed magic to invade the realm of incipient science, to overlay it and conceal it, even to the point of making us all believe in a primitive mentality devoid of all real science. (Bergson 1935, 162 [1932, 182])

We must admit that, hidden in the sorcery of primitives, there is consummate knowledge of remedies and poisons necessarily acquired through much observation. However, this knowledge of herbs has not progressed. On the contrary, among Africans today it is not the juices of the plant in themselves that kill or cure, but the rite that makes them sacred. Once there may have been the embryo of medical science, but it was smothered when magic superimposed itself. The same applies to all other techniques. As both Weber and Allier note, irresistible magic has "made men lose the benefits of discoveries to which a reasonable empiricism had led them."

If we want to find traces of magical thought today, we should not look to science but to music and poetry, where we may find its last reflections. If, as we have tried to establish, incantation is, according to Allier, the very root of magic, it is important to have, as the Egyptians said, "the right voice," for it is the voice that brings forth occult powers. Magic is "frozen music" (Combarieu). Autolycos's son's singing stanches the blood flowing from Ulysses' wound; Orpheus calms the beasts; Joshua makes the walls of Jericho fall; and the Hindus, like the Chinese, have their ragas (chants), each linked with a season of the year and intended to ensure the proper progression of the sun or the correct rainfall. For example, when Akber wanted to sing the raga of night at noon, darkness fell for as far as his voice carried. What is true of music is also true of poetry: there is no poem without meter and the explanation of the notion of *meter* is not complete so long as it has not been "compared to that of *foot*, which can only be done if one agrees to remember the kinship between poetry, music, orchestration, chanted verse and dance; and no one can ignore the kinship between dance and magic" (Richard). Romance results from the love charm and the epic from the myth, the recitation of which provides the rhythm for the magical ceremony and the drama of the rite. The links that united magic and poetry relax little by little. As a civilization develops, it places more importance on higher abstract thinking, to the detriment of music and images. Yet, poetry will always retain something of its distant origins, unless it ceases to be poetry. It will keep the rhythm, the dancing play of musical analogies, the subtle correspondences, the mysterious power that tears us away from real life to plunge us into another existence, a secret one, full of unexpected resonance.

In summary, what prolongs the existence of ancient magic in present society is not science, but the phonic arts.

We have seen that magic cannot be the ancestor of science because it manipulates sacred forces and uses mystical properties. Thus it is closer to religion. We now come to the main issue, the one we stated at the end of the previous chapter, which is that of the relations between religion and magic and their respective definitions.

First, we could consider magic to be a counterreligion or a reverse religion, which instead of addressing good powers to pray to them, summons evil beings to use them to achieve the blackest plans. According to this thesis, religion would be primitive, magic derived. This is Jevons's opinion.

It contains an element of truth. Sorcery often presents itself as the reverse copy of official religion. This is the case of the Christian Sabbath, but the "black mass" is a more general phenomenon that can be found elsewhere than in the West. In Vedic India there was a magical sacrifice that was the opposite of one in the Brahman religion. Trilles, who compared Fan cultural ceremonies with those of their sorcerers, pinpointed their opposition clearly. The latter take place at night, seek obscenity and cruelty, not religious fervor, and are reached by flying through the air, just as in the case of the Western black Sabbath.

However, this theory leaves aside the existence of a whole other magic: the licit, official magic, which, far from being the opposite of the religion, is instead its indispensable auxiliary. In Egypt, magicians received their formulas from the gods, from Thoth and Khonsu. The Osirification of the king was a magical ceremony, since it was by imitating the death and resurrection of Osiris that the pharaoh became a god. Yet this rite was directed by a priest. Assyrian magic was also created by the gods Ea and Marduk. Demons played no role in it except as forces to be fought against; thus the magician had an official role and a high rank in the cult. In Vedic India, the magician protected the sacrifice from evil spirits that could disturb it. Among savages, a sorcerer is often a real "civil servant" who is responsible for making rain fall if there is a drought, revealing the guilty party if there is a crime, and preparing charms when there is an expedition.

This theory also neglects the fact that next to ceremonial, demonic magic, there is much simpler, natural magic. Indeed, this magic seems to us to be more primitive. Originally, magic was neither a caricature of, nor, at least in its initial forms, posterior to religion.

Would it not instead be prior? This opinion was defended by Frazer, who spoke of an age "of magic," as we normally speak of the Stone Age. Religion supposes belief in personal agents and gods, notions too complex to have been born in the brain of a primitive, while magic supposes only the imperfect application of more simple mental principles and the laws of the association of ideas. Thus it is theoretically more plausible "that magic arose before religion in the evolution of our race, and that man essayed to bend nature to his wishes by the sheer force of spells and enchantments before he strove to coax and mollify a coy, capricious, or irascible deity by the soft insinuation of prayer and sacrifice" (Frazer 1957, 72).

This thesis is attractive, but only hypothetical. It is based on psychology alone, on the simplicity of imaginative association in opposition to the complexity of conceptualization. Yet we must examine the facts: neither Howitt nor Frazer found religion among the Australians, whom they thought were the people with the least developed mental abilities, and it is clear that among the Australians magic covers almost everything. However, later research determined that belief in great gods, creators and fathers, is found in Australia, and this is at least the embryo of a religion.

Neither history nor ethnography allows us to establish any sort of sequential relationship between magic and religion. They have always coexisted and continue to coexist everywhere.

However, the essential question has not yet been answered. If they both act in the domain of the sacred, what separates them?

Shall we say that religion is licit and magic forbidden? Yet in addition to criminal rituals, such as bewitchment, there are the rituals of the sorcerer who is a public servant and works for the cult to protect the tribe from demons and to make rain fall. Shall we say that magic is characterized by belief in impersonal forces, by the idea that things have mystical properties, whereas religion is characterized by faith in individual gods? Yet, as we have seen, there is indirect magic that supposes the existence of deities and, reciprocally, religion that surrounds itself with taboos and prohibitions, consequences of the recognition of impersonal occult powers. Shall we say that the action of a magical ritual is inevitable, that nature or a god is forced to submit to the orders of the sorcerer, while religion is worship, submission, and prayer? This would be to forget that many religious rites, for example Vedic sacrifice, also act mechanically and that magic sometimes also requires prayer and sacrifice. Finally, shall we say that religion is the church, the community of the faithful, united in a common undertaking, whereas magic is a separate society in which individual goals take precedence over those that are shared? Yet in accomplishing his rites, an African fetishist has the support of the whole tribe, and he feels he is their representative and responsible for them.

However, while the antithetical definitions thus proposed are false when they are suggested in the sphere of concepts, they ring true when they are transposed into the domain of evolution. Perhaps it could be said that they have never been completely accurate, but tend to become more so as we go from savage to civilized peoples. In consequence, we can say of them that which is said of sociological laws: they indicate directions rather than describe rules. They are *definitions of tendencies*.

Above all, as Hubert and Mauss say, religion *tends* toward the pole of sacrifice and magic toward that of evil. This evolution can be seen in antiquity, but culminates in Christianity. Christianity inherited Roman law, which maintained, while imposing its own spirit on, barbarian laws that punished all evil spells, witches, and poisoners. Thus a condemnation that fell under public law and was intended as a protection against criminal attacks also fell under religious law: crime was also sacrilege.

Religion *tends* toward the pious worship of deities and increasingly rejects the action of impersonal mystical forces. The ritual is no longer sufficient: it must also be performed with a pure heart. Magic, on the contrary, retains the use of incantation, imitation, and contagion. Later it probably adds demons, but even when it addresses individual beings, they are not those of the official religion.

Here we see, by way of parenthesis, that while like Durkheim we believe in the existence of primitive religions, in nonanimist sacred rites, we cannot believe that great atheist religions could arise in our time. For example, we do not consider Buddhism a religion: it is a philosophy, certainly a moral and emotional philosophy, but a philosophy all the same. "It was only when, in contradiction with its first principles, it made its founder into a god" (Tiele) in response to the requirements of popular enthusiasm and when it integrated the spirits of the woods, the waters, and the mountains into its master doctrine that it became a religion.

Religion *tends* toward offerings and prayer. Magic remains a pure operative mechanism, and if it also becomes spiritual, fasting, virtue, and chastity will not operate as moral virtues, but as mystical properties. They prevent the loss of magical powers and increase mental concentration, the creator of miracles.

Religion *tends* toward a community of the faithful. Even when it is most individualistic, as in the Anglo-Saxon countries, it cannot do without churches. It rejects individual goals and egotistical pursuit of salvation. On the contrary, magic increasingly individualizes its practitioners and loses all its communal aspects. Huvelin has provided a striking example of this in the study of law. While internal social law, such as family law and public law, has its roots in religion, law protecting persons and individual property has its roots in magic. The *tabellae defixionum* (from *defigere*) are curses that owners use against thieves to enchant them until the spoils are returned.

All such antagonistic tendencies are implied in the very essence of religion and magic. They are not created or the results of conquests, but are the progressive clarification of an opposition of kind.

Where does this lead us? Since these two forms of the sacred cannot both triumph simultaneously, one must necessarily win out over the other.

We know of no people that is ignorant of magic. However, it is developed to different degrees throughout the globe. Pygmies, the Eskimos of the Barren Grounds, Koryks, and Algonquins seem, according to recent research, to know of only the simplest forms of magic, while they believe in powerful protective gods.[1] From this point of departure, two lines diverge: one leads to peoples among whom religion repulses magic and surrounds it with strict limitations, and the other leads to peoples among whom magic smothers religion and invades the whole area of the sacred.

This is one of the most curious phenomena in the sociology of religion: the separation of two humanities, one ascending toward divine worship and the other mummifying itself in the complications of magical ritual. How can this schism be explained and what must have happened "at the crossroads" (Allier)?

Psychological causes might first spring to mind. Colonial doctors spoke of excitability, mythomania and suggestibility among noncivilized people. Indeed, we find in the mentally ill the beginnings of magical formulas and techniques: in order to get rid of his obsessions, one patient was obliged to repeat, "five times five equals twenty-

five, I am the Queen of France Zarzi imprisoned in Sal-
pêtrière Hospital"; a child was sure he would get a good
mark in class if he arrived at the end of the school yard
before the door closed; and a little girl engaged in the
mimetic rite of chewing rose petals in order to achieve a
rosy complexion. These examples, borrowed from Allier,
are sufficient to reveal the beginnings of magical behavior
among mental patients. Thus we could look for the solution to our problem in psychiatry, which is what Freud
tried to do. If, he said, magic is born of the omnipotence
of ideas, then it shares that characteristic with the principle of obsessive mental illness: patients make their fan-
tasies come true just as do primitives their desires.

We cannot deny that an individual's physical constitution is important. Yet we cannot make whole peoples
out to be candidates for institutionalization. Thus we must
look elsewhere. Frazer seems to lean toward climate;
Allier, toward moral causes, such as laziness, sensuality,
and sexual violence; and Schmidt, toward social causes:

> Totemic civilization presents us with two factors that
> stimulate the development of active magic. The first is
> made up of a whole series of technical achievements in the
> manufacturing of hunting tools. . . . This made men aware
> of their strength. . . . From then on . . . they began to look
> for ways and means to control other people and the forces
> of nature, even to the point of using their most virile
> aspects: their reproductive power. The second factor was
> the importance of the tribe. . . . For the first time the
> disturbing, paralyzing influence of the crowd came to have
> power over judgments, emotions, and behavior. Passive
> magic developed with small-scale farming and matriarchy

because of the "more fearful, passive nature of women"
and especially because of "random events in such farming,
where success depends more on the favorable succession
of seasons than on human industry."

Whether or not this is correct, there is a whole series of peoples among whom magic has progressed by increasing its power and extending its domain. These peoples are those that Lévy-Bruhl has described most luminously. His picture is not that of primitive mentality, properly speaking, but of peoples who have frozen themselves in magic.

This explains the standstill of the noncivilized. Magic has taken them out of the stage of primitive humanity only to immobilize them forever in its sacred swathes. Discoveries of prehistoric pottery and drawings prove that the first men had a thrilling vitality, a creative youth, "a vigorous, winning, flexible freshness.... We must be careful not to confuse expiring hardened tired beings with those still tender and full of potential, who were the authentic roots" (Le Roy). However, magic, by imprisoning them in superstitions that took all their power from respect for formulas, transformed them into mummies.

The end of technological development: initiative and progress are eliminated and thought is constrained. The end of moral effort: "the natural candor of the mind" is darkened to make way for shared fears and the reign of desires instead of the will, passion instead of reason. The truth of this is such that, while magic kills morals, morals in turn kill magic. To limit ourselves to one example, Egypt reveals this reciprocal, antithetical action: the intervention of magic in the popular religion of death annihilated the first seeds of piety, but among the elite, magic also gradually gave way to morality, and immortality became the fruit not of a rite, but of the judgment of sins.

In summary, there is probably a stage at which magic and religion are not yet separated, but where the struggle is already sketched. Then there is the crossroads between the route toward "sleeping immobility" and that toward spirituality, as if there were, at the beginning of history, an act of freedom. Or, to avoid metaphysics, an act of choice, but such a choice would of course be governed by psychology (excessive excitability), technology (farmers and hunters), and morphology (tribal organization).

Part II. Social Elements of Religious Life

Religion is first emotion and life. It is so for the primitive who, through the appropriate rituals, pulls away from the profane world to penetrate the sacred domain, which is normally forbidden. It is so for our contemporaries, whether they bow their heads under the broad gestures of the priest or kneel before their god in the silence of their rooms.

Yet every life, even the most solitary and voluntarily removed from religious authority, tends, if it is intense, to lead to intellectual beliefs and to actions. While emotion is something individual, our thoughts and actions can be communicated, set in words, and expressed in rituals, and thus can take on a social aspect. Perhaps later people will no longer use the same words to signify the same experiences and will pour new emotions into the same ritual frameworks. Yet concrete expressions of emotions will still survive, impose themselves, and then provide the social frameworks of religious experience.

From the outside, we cannot penetrate to the very interior of what is religion, yet the study of such forms remains singularly captivating in itself. It is the primary goal of the sociology of religion.

CHAPTER 3

Representational Elements

Elementary Representations

Primitive thought is not yet completely free of animal instinct. It "aims at action" rather than contemplation, and is "in action rather than in thought" (Bergson 1935, 155). Thus among primitives we do not find well-defined, clear intellectual representations, sharply delineated hierarchical notions, or theological systems. Instead we find only spontaneous psychological reactions to things: intellectual attitudes. As Bergson says: "Before any man can philosophize, he must live. Original dispositions and convictions must have sprung from a vital necessity. . . . [The primitive mind] simply translates the suggestions of instinct into ideas."

However, as man has succeeded in dominating nature and in consequence becoming free of it, he has had more time to reflect, and thus, when we consider savage peoples today, we find an intermediary situation, of semimotor, semireflective representations.

This has two consequences:

First, it is vain to try to determine which religious concepts are primitive and which are derived—in other words, to try to reconstitute in the fashion of Tylor or Wundt the intellectual evolution of humanity. Which concept is prior, spirit or mana? Always and everywhere we find them indissolubly linked, and nothing enables us to determine their date of birth or civil status. All genealogies, however painstaking or complex, are houses of cards that tumble as soon as they are built!

Moreover, we must be careful not to define these notions too precisely or to be ready to pay any price to see even a naive or absurd system in the formulae. It is good to leave a fringe of uncertainty and a halo of confusion around primitive religious concepts.

Among such concepts, sociologists customarily distinguish those that designate impersonal forces (mana) from those that designate personal spirits. Perhaps this distinction goes too far. Nonetheless we will use it as our point of departure.

The Notion of Mana

The term *mana*, borrowed from the Melanesians, was introduced into sociology by Codrington and Tregear. They used it in the sense of a magical power, "altogether distinct from any physical power, which acts in all kinds of ways, for good and evil, and which it is of the greatest advantage to possess or control" (Codrington 1891, 118).

Since Codrington's discovery, many analogous terms have been noted in virtually all peoples. Among the Papuans, the Madagascans *(hasina)*, the Ewe (*dzô*, more accurately magical, and *tro*, more accurately religious), and the Ba-Ronga (*Tilo*, usually the sky, which is also synonymous with impersonal power). In short, the notion of mystical power is so widespread in Africa that Kingsley goes so far as to see African fetishism as a kind of primitive pantheism and a savage Spinozism. However, the most interesting similarities are found mainly in America.

Among the Tlingit, there is the *yêk*, a spiritual power that is distinct from natural energy but has an impersonal nature and takes a personal form when it appears to people. Among the Haida, there is the more personified *sgâna*. Among the Lango there is *jok*, an extremely complex notion that sometimes designates an impersonal power, a sort of breath making the life of the community possible; sometimes the supreme being; sometimes a mysterious reality identical with individual souls; sometimes the spirits of the ancestors taken collectively; sometimes also the power used by a sorcerer; and so on. Among the Omaha there is the *wakenda*, which includes "all secret power, all that is divine" (Riggs). Among the Hurons, there is the *orenda*, which Hewitt defines as "a mysterious power that the savage conceives as inherent in all bodies making up the environment in which he lives . . . , in rocks, waterways, plants, trees, animals and men, winds and storms, clouds, thunder, lightning."

It is said that the remnants of this concept could even be seen among the ancients. The Egyptians had *ka*, the force of nature, life of animals and mind of man, a primordial and universal substance that could also individualize itself in specialized properties. The Romans had *sacer*, the Hebrews *el*. Finally, there is the North African idea of *baraka*, a sacred fluid that is secreted by the marabout and spreads into everything that touches the saintly man such as his clothes and bathwater, survives in his corpse, and remains with his tomb. Thus ethnography, like history, would seem to prove the generality of a notion of impersonal power, to which sociologists customarily give the generic name of "mana."

Unfortunately, the first to observe this idea, Codrington, probably perceived it through the theories of his teacher, Max Müller, who considered the source of religion to be in the perception of the infinite. He was thus led to make it "something abstract and metaphysical" (Söderblom), far from the true thought of primitives. Since then, this notion has given rise to more detailed and critical studies (particularly the work of Lehmann), which have enabled many preconceived ideas to be eliminated.

First, while the notion of mana can be religious, it does not seem to be so by definition. Söderblom already related it to ideas, such as the astonishing, the bizarre, and the very strong, that are just as secular as they are sacred. For Lehmann, the word is neutral and can in consequence be applied to various types of power or authority, both natural and supernatural. Likewise, "in addition to the meaning of sacred, *wakenda* and *manitou* also mean rare, unusual, and powerful, without the slightest allusion to the presence of an inherent force, but simply in the ordinary sense of these adjectives" (Radin).

Moreover, we must not think of an impersonal force included in all natural objects or in only some of them: "[T]he natives certainly never told Codrington that mana was impersonal," Hocart writes, "because they could never have conceived of such an idea." Of course *mana* can designate special objects that emit mystical power (the excrement of sorcerers, for example), but this is a secondary idea, which could have arisen only after the fact. Thus mana that is external is objectivized (in the case of defecation, this is the sorcerer's mana). This point of view is not far from the idea of an impersonal fluid. However, once again, this notion is revealed late, and the linguistic data gathered by Lehmann show clearly that the primary meaning of *mana* is that of a personal power, a warrior's, hunter's, ancestor's, chief's, or priest's power, a human power that is very distant from the mechanical power of a magic ritual or the power of spirits and the dead. Here the power is supernatural and suprasensible, but always personal. The same seems to apply for the similar notions held by Indians.

However, while the primitive meaning of *mana* does not seem to be an impersonal, mystical power, this is nevertheless the meaning into which it evolves among many peoples.

We do not have enough space to identify the various lines of its evolution. We will content ourselves with indicating the main ones.

Durkheim and Saintyves tried to see in the idea of mana the first form of the idea of energy, which plays such a major role in modern physics. The transition between these two concepts would be provided by the notion of *physis* or the Stoic *dynamis*, a notion half mystical and half scientific. However, we saw earlier the difficulties facing a thesis that makes science the true continuation of magic.

We prefer to look for the still recognizable successors of Polynesian mana in Paracelsus's *Magnale*, Fludd's *Magnetica virtus*, and Wirdig's magnetism—in short, in the ideas of modern occultists.

Söderblom and Hubert and Mauss have shed light on another evolutionary process, which will gradually lead us from mana to religious pantheism. Vedic India had two notions very similar to that of mana: the notion of Brahma, which indicates the power of incantations and rituals, as well as the power of sorcerers, and the notion of atman, which designates vital human force as well as the creative power at work in the universe. Next, in the Upanishad, we see these two notions overlap to finally merge so that Brahma then designates the mysterious substance inherent in things. Söderblom also recognizes the Iranian Mithra, a product of parallel evolutions, in the Hvarenah of the Avesta. An analogous systematization, though somewhat less developed, can also be seen among the Annamites, who make the *tin-khi* a sort of soul of the universe.

Souls and Spirits

What characterizes the soul in modern theology and metaphysics is its unity and absolute simplicity. It was not always this way, and what emerges from contemporary ethnographic work is, on the contrary, the original complexity of this notion. Among the Laotians, the same individual can have up to thirty souls. While not usually going to this extreme, noncivilized people generally distinguish the following, according to the documents of explorers and missionaries:

1. The soul of the body. After death, a corpse retains a phantom existence, at least so long as it is not decomposed. This gives rise to two series of actions. One consists in breaking the limbs, fracturing the bones, and encouraging the decomposition of the corpse because of fear of the dead, frightening ghosts that haunt nightmares and cause calamities. The other consists, on the contrary, in drying out and mummifying the corpse to make it last as long as

possible, caring for it and providing it with food, drink, and slaves so that it will survive as long as possible in the night of the tomb.

2. The specialized souls. In addition to phantoms, there can be a whole series of vital principles linked to the various organs of the body. The fat of the kidneys, the heart, the liver, the entrails, the toe among peoples used to walking long distances, the phallus, and hot blood thus become the home of specialized souls.

3. The soul-breath. This was the *psyche* for the Greeks, and its legacy to us was the transition from the idea of a vital principle to that of a spirit. However, breath is first conceived of as a material reality, and the ancients often represented it in the form of a bird or butterfly.

4. The external soul. "[T]he savage thinks of it as a concrete material thing of a definite bulk, capable of being seen and handled, kept in a box or jar, and liable to be bruised, fractured, or smashed in pieces. . . . there may be circumstances in which, if the life or soul remains in the man, it stands a greater chance of sustaining injury than if it were stowed away in some safe and secret place. Accord-ingly, . . . primitive man takes his soul out of his body and deposits it for security in some snug spot" (Frazer 1957, 874). For example, it is kept in a bag at Minahassa; else-where in a hatchet; in a piece of wood, the *churinga*, in Australia; but most often in a plant or animal (werewolf, crocodile, spirit of the forest, *nagual*, etc.). Of course, when the animal is killed or the object destroyed, the man mys-tically linked to it dies ipso facto.

5. The shadow. The non- or half-civilized considers his shadow to be his soul; "if it is trampled upon, struck

or stabbed, he will feel the injury as if it were done to his person; and if it is detached from him entirely (as he believes that it may be) he will die" (Frazer 1957, 250).

6. The name. This is also an integral part of an individual's personality. The Eskimos define it as "a sort of soul with which a certain amount of vitality and skill is associated"; for the ancient Chinese, says Granet, "the name . . . was identical to the superior soul, to destiny, to life itself." In the Egyptian sanctuary of Edfou there is the following inscription: "May the gods reward you if you speak my name." He whose name is spoken lives.

These various "selves" should not be considered separate substances. They often interact and lend themselves to much confusion. Yet they have developed in different directions.

By analyzing the Arunta totemists, the Bampangu manists, and the Kwakiutl Indians, Larock showed that the name was losing more and more of its sacred value to become only a social sign, the testimony of rank in society, approximately "what is for us the possession of civil and political rights." Likewise, in the vitalist doctrines that the Montpellier school of medicine perhaps inherited from Jewish or Arab doctors, we can see the remnants of the "soul of the living," or vital principles, transmitted through medieval mystics. Finally, the corporeal soul, "that vaporous, elusive image that persisted after death, a feeble impotent shadow . . . , due to its tenuousness, even its quasi immateriality," opened the way, according to the best Hellenists, to "the path to spirituality." This was done either directly, through gradual transitions (Weil), or more bru-tally, through the Dionysian and Orphic cult in which the physical counterpart gives way to a more spiritual reality, one closer to the gods, which is imprisoned in the body but can emerge when one is in a trance (Rhode). In these three cases, there has been secularization and laicization. Yet even today the notion of soul has not lost its mystical origins. By its survival, its links to the divine, and the role it plays in religious dogma, the soul clearly retains its na-ture as a religious representation.

Natural spirits, which people the forests, stir up the waters, and scream in the wind, are closely related to the disembodied souls with which they are most often gradu-ally confused in primitive thought. This is why we should talk about them here. Such spirits are identified only by their functions or their special places of residence. How-ever, their nature is generally vague and their contours indistinct. They still live, with faded outlines, in the mem-ories of elders in the countryside.

There are air demons, stormy winds that lead savage dances; water spirits, with deceitful charms and sudden wrath; familiar domestic spirits that are in many countries intimately linked to the souls of the ancestors; spirits of the earth, such as giants and elves; demons of illness that cause delirium and fever; and especially spirits of plants, such as barley and wheat, trees and flowers.

However, above this vast crowd in the immensity of the world, there are the gods, engaged in a whole series of adventures. With them and behind them, we penetrate into the domain of myths.

Myths

Myths have been defined in a number of ways. Sometimes it is said that they report the stories of gods, just as legends report those of heroes. However, there is no insurmountable abyss between gods and heroes. Heroes are the offspring of deities and when they die they join the immortals. They are also often worshiped. Sometimes myth is also defined by its timeless nature, whereas a folktale or legend takes place at a certain date, but this is merely a relatively external feature. Thus we will instead consider the following definition: a myth is an object of belief. It is about the gods, the world, human relations with the supernatural, and a whole set of ideas that vary in detail but have a sufficiently stable framework, are adopted by a group of some size, and form for that group a primary credo. We will come back to this point.

Myths are complex wholes in which a certain number of themes can be identified. For example, the Semitic narrative of the flood includes five themes: God wants to punish corrupt humanity, a pious man receives an order to build a ship, he brings onboard animals of each species, he releases a dove, and he lands on a high mountain (according to Usener). A "thematic cycle" is such a combination of themes. When many myths are compared with each other, it can be seen that a number of thematic cycles on the same subject include very different themes along with the ones they share and, reciprocally, that a single theme can be found in thematic cycles that are otherwise unrelated.

We must not allow ourselves to be hypnotized, as some people have been, by considering themes alone, for, even among primitive peoples, nothing is found in isolation. "We should not attribute a real existence to the distinctions drawn by scientific analysis. In real life, only prior syntheses are available for observation" (Van Gennep). Thus what is important is the order in which such themes are arranged in relation to each other, in other words, the schema of the myth, the "thematic sequence."

Myths have given rise to two sciences: comparative mythology, which studies myths within a single racial branch, for example all Indo-European myths, and universal mythology, which explores the whole world. We do not have room here to describe the results of these two approaches. Since we are concerned only with the sociology of religion, we must confine ourselves to showing only the following:

> that myths are religious representations, and
> that these religious representations are shared
> representations.[1]

First we will discuss the thesis that myths are religious representations. There is a whole series of thinkers who try to separate mythology from religion. Some, like Le Roy, who focuses mainly on naturalist myths that use great imagery to describe celestial and terrestrial phenomena, want to see in them an initial form of science. This is an opinion that has often been held, from the time of the ancient Stoics to the Pan-Babylonists to today. Siecke and Lessmann, for example, consider myths to represent "childish but serious judgments and questions about the marvels of nature surrounding humanity."

Others, such as Wundt, see such narratives as mere poetry and entertainment. Certainly, magical beliefs and popular superstitions can play a role in them from time to time, but they are nonetheless essentially the work of artistic imagination. They belong more to aesthetics than to religion. Contrary to popular belief, which considers tales to be the survivors of ancient religious myths, Wundt notes the grotesque or comical nature of many Australian tales and therefore considers stories to be the more primitive form. The myth of the gods would be nothing but a promotion of human legend. According to him, the evolution of human mythology occurs in the following manner:

> First there are simple associations of images, that of life, for example, leaving the body of a dying person and that of a snake slithering along the ground near the dead person's hut (metempsychosis).
>
> Then there are more complicated fables, entertainment for old women and children, such as totemic fables.
>
> Next there are myths, which try to explain natural phenomena, but soon go beyond simple explanation to lean toward poetry.
>
> This is followed by the legends of heroes.
>
> Finally there are myths in the proper sense of the word, adventures of the gods that simply idealize human exploits and which are, like legends, the work of poets, historians, and artists. Since the gods are also the objects of religious beliefs and worship,

mythology becomes amalgamated with religion. Yet, as can be seen, this is a secondary fact and is, so to speak, external to the very spirit of mythology.

These hypotheses certainly contain a large portion of truth. Humans put their whole selves into myths, including their minds, which seek explanations, and their imagination, sensitivity to poetry, and also religious emotion.

The Australians probably do tell amusing tales, but "these stories are numerous only where the former social organization (totemic system and classification marriage system) has lost its authority: Queensland, New South Wales" (Van Gennep). Thus they seem to be nothing more than transformations of old beliefs that are in the process of disappearing. While there are some stories in the most primitive tribes (Arunta, Dieri), we must immediately note that they are left to women and children and that, in addition to these exoteric tales, there are others reserved for men and revealed at initiation. While the same thematic sequence can belong to both categories, can be both a myth and a tale, that proves only that these two types of narrative are simultaneous and not, as Wundt believes, that tales are prior to myths.

Myth essentially seems to be a religious fact.

It is a religious fact primarily because it is an object of belief. Among many peoples, mythical narratives are taught to young people during initiation ceremonies, along with the secret names of the gods and traditional customs, in other words a complete sacred heritage, the possession of which distinguishes adults from children. These revelations make up a sort of primitive catechism, to which one must subscribe with one's heart and mind and of which, in consequence, it is impossible to deny the religious nature.

Next it is a religious fact because, even if poetry does play a role in it along with individual whims, myth remains bound to rite. This was first demonstrated by Bérard in his book, *L'origine des cultes arcadiens.* Myth is born of rite; it is simply ritual's translation into ideas and images. For example, the myth of Lycaon giving his own son to be devoured by Zeus has its source in the fact that children were sacrificed to the Lycaonian Zeus. This was the point of departure for a whole line of research that resulted in emphasizing mythology's linkages to ritual and thus to its religious meaning. We will limit ourselves to two examples. The first is taken from an agrarian civilization, the second from an urban one.

Among all Indo-Europeans there is a legend of ambrosia that can be summarized in the following way: the hungry gods make ambrosia, elixir of immortality, by churning the contents of the vat formed by the sea. However, a demon steals the precious drink, so a god takes the form of a woman and charms the demon in order to get the ambrosia back. A fight follows and the gods finish triumphant. This legend supposes a certain number of prior rituals that can be found preserved, at least in part, in the Latin festival of Anna Perenna, in the Armenian celebration of spring, in the Thargelies, and so on. A certain ritual drink is prepared in a vat, a man representing a demon steals it and is then expelled (flagellation rituals).

There is a communion through consumption of food, such as a banquet in the fields. A man disguised as a woman is paraded carrying a goblet of the drink. Two groups joust and wrestle, and there are rituals of sexual union. What the seasonal feasts explain about the legend are the two themes of the god disguised as a woman and the expulsion and killing of the demon thief. Indeed, disguises and killings characterize carnivals, May festivals, and all agrarian ceremonies: the mannequin represents the old vegetation that the winter has killed to make way for the spring plants. The wearing of disguises followed by sexual rituals is intended to enhance, through imitative magic, the fertility of the fields. Light can be shed on ambrosia through the American institution of the potlatch. Potlatches are sumptuous communal feasts that one clan offers another, which is obliged to return the service, and where challenges are exchanged between rivals. In the myth we see, as in the potlatch, two clans (gods and demons) entering into competition over magical food and power acquired through victory in food-related contests. Thus "it is as if the ambrosia cycle translated a springtime festival into a legend in which the central episode is a sort of potlatch of beer" (Dumézil).

If we turn from agrarian civilizations to urban ones, the fundamental ritual is that of the construction of cities. For that purpose, a belt of trenches was dug, on which walls were then constructed. This ceremony was commemorated each year by circumambulation, such as the *amburbian* in Rome and the *hib Sokar* in Egypt. When danger arose, Christianity did not abolish the custom. To renew the mystical strength of the city, this solemn procession was repeated. It enveloped the walls and covered them with its protective, prophylactic virtue. However, there was a countermagic, the goal of which was to destroy a magical action by repeating it, but in reverse, beginning with the end and continuing in the opposite direction. This procedure made it possible to use the circumambulation ritual to achieve completely opposite goals: all that was required was that the direction of the movement be reversed. Thus, the Scottish considered the Deasil, or circumambulation in the direction of the sun, as beneficial, but the Withershin, which was performed in the opposite direction, as harmful. In his *Folklore biblique*, Saintyves uses these data on rites to explain the legend of Joshua circling the city of Jericho three times in order to take possession of it.

However, this theory should not be overgeneralized. While the myth of the suffering, dying god, for example that of Osiris, is sometimes related to a sacrificial rite that can allow the god to recover, "we know of no divine sacrificial rites for Orpheus, Hippolyte, Marsyas, or Acteon" (Hubert). There is also a fertile flowering of myths around the Titans and Tethys, though neither Tethys nor the Titans were worshiped.

Many rites, moreover, are far from primitive and express prior mythical beliefs. We cannot understand many actions, attitudes, and ceremonies if we do not accept the prior existence of a certain number of ideas that are already sufficiently clear. To limit ourselves to one example, beliefs about the beyond cannot be born of expiatory rituals. On the contrary, these rituals can be explained as attempts at imitating the legends and narratives of the great adventure in the realm beyond.

Whether myth is born of ritual or ritual is produced by myth, there is a relation between the two, and that is sufficient for our thesis.

What remains from Wundt's conception is that not all religions contain myths, that pantheism or speculative monotheism, for example, is incompatible with them, and that mythology flourishes freely only in the anthropomorphic religions, where the gods are conceived of as having human form.

What remains is also that myths allow for the workings of fantasy. They provide a special realm for the poet's gifts, but even when fantasy takes over myth, all the links with religion are not broken:

> As practical as religion may be, pure representation has a large role to play in it. To leave a myth outside of religion, to fail to use it to nourish piety and provide meaning to rituals, appears to us not only to diminish religion, but to impoverish it.... Religion cannot do without the imagination, but *the imagination that serves it is religious.* (Hubert)

Finally, while in the major religions myths can acquire lyrical independence, among the most primitive peoples, where they continue to play their proper role, they are not simply narratives: they are action. We must not forget that words have magical value. The word causes the sun to rise in the east, attracts the moon's canoe in the night sky, and recreates the trembling life of nature each spring. Myths, which are compilations of words, produce actions simply by expressing them. Among the Huichols, the pattern of a myth is that of a prayer.

However, it is not only because they are religious representations that myths should give us pause: it is of course also because they are shared representations.[2]

We do not mean to say by this that society creates myths. It simply conditions the elaboration of themes and writes itself, with its own forms, into the narrative or legend. The best studied such case is that of the combat between father and son that Potter reported in an important book. Potter takes the story of Sohrab and Rustem as his point of departure. Rustem is off hunting wild donkeys and comes to Semengam, where he is received by the king. During the night he is visited by the daughter of the king, Tehmineh, who gives herself to him. Nine months later Sohrab is born; when he is ten, he asks about the secret of his birth. Sohrab then sets off with an army to meet his father and encounters him unknowingly because Rustem is hiding his identity. The result is that Sohrab is killed. Analogous myths can be found in New Zealand (the story of Kokako), in Guyana among the Arawaks, among the Irish (the Epic of Cuchulainn), among the Greeks (Ulysses and Telegone, Oedipus), among the Scandinavians (An and Drisa, Bui and Fridr), and in India (Arjuna and Chitrangrada).

The explanation of origin of this strange story could be that the myth simply expresses a specific social structure. The first theme, that of the hero's long trip, supposes that the father takes a wife outside of the group to which he belongs; in other words, it is a case of exogamy. The second theme, that of the nocturnal visit, shows a woman in charge of her destiny and not blindly subject to male power. She is able to choose her husband; thus it is a case of matriarchy. The third theme, in which the father leaves for new adventures far away, indicates temporary marriages. The fourth theme, that of the child who leaves to find his father, demonstrates not a matriarchy, but the passage of the child into a patriarchy. For the child to seek his father so actively, there must be something binding them together that the child considers very important. Paternity must already play an important role, in comparison with that of maternity, in the shared ideas of the society where the legend is born.

Thus, myths reflect social structures. However, they also have sociological interest because they play one of the most important roles in communities.

What is this role? In order to identify it, Bergson begins with a very simple observation: animals have no religion. What characterizes them is the strength of their instinct. Yet sociability can be seen in its highest forms among hymenopteran insects (ants and bees) and among humans. However, among the former it is set and immutable, while among the latter it changes. This opposition definitely rests on the opposition between instinct and intelligence. Instinct conserves and maintains, while intelligence, an analytical and distinguishing faculty, destroys. Therefore,

> [i]f intelligence now threatens to break up social cohesion at certain points—assuming that society is to go on—there must be a counterpoise, at these points, to intelligence. If this counterpoise cannot be instinct itself, for the very reason that its place has been taken by intelligence, the

> same effect must be produced by a virtuality of instinct,
> or, if you prefer it, by the residue of instinct which
> survives on the fringe of intelligence: it cannot exercise
> direct action, but, since intelligence works on representa-
> tions, it will call up imaginary ones, which will hold their
> own against the representation of reality and will succeed,
> through the agency of intelligence itself, in counteract-
> ing the work of intelligence. This would be the expla-
> nation of the myth-making faculty. (Bergson 1935, 109
> [1932, 124])

In the beehive or anthill, the animal has only to follow its instinct for the community to be able to survive and overcome any danger threatening to destroy it. In human society, in contrast, intelligence risks turning people in on themselves, causing them to lose interest in others and teaching them egoism. However, nature is watching over us, and what remains of the social instinct in humans causes the ghost of a defending, threatening, and repressive god to spring up against destructive intelligence to protect the city. Imagination will then be able to elaborate on the initial themes and create a whole moral mythology of the gods pursuing the guilty and protecting ancient customs. The origin of this veritable defensive reflex will be the need to preserve human society.

Finally, myths are social facts owing to their generality. There are without doubt individual variants, but overall, myths are believed by groups of various sizes and are the shared heritage of various numbers of people. Some legends can be found everywhere, such as that of the flood. Others are strictly local and exist only in a very small area. Finally, there are veritable thematic provinces.

However, these provinces do not, according to Van Gennep, correspond to cultural divisions. In other words, myths become disconnected from their social milieus and emigrate to other areas, where they lead independent lives. Soldiers, caravans, slaves, missionaries, and explorers carry with them the stories of their home countries, and those stories are adopted by very distant cultures. Thus Indian myths have infiltrated the Malaysian archipelago, China, and even Japan. According to Dahnhardt, Persian dualism can be found even in North America. The Pan-Babylonian school has even had the pretension to claim that Babylon was the unique point of departure for all mythology. This is clearly an exaggeration, but myths, like "rolling stones," can travel very far. This uprooting is accentuated even more when peoples intermix, such as when there are major invasions, empires fall, and savages are driven out of their original homelands.

Let us stop here. Indeed, when a myth breaks all ties with a social structure or specific civilization and goes off to live an independent life, and when it becomes prey for poets and the canvas on which imaginative fantasy embroiders, it ceases to belong to sociology and becomes the object of a new field of study, that of myths.

Dogmas

With the great universal religions, such as Christianity, Buddhism, and Islam, we see the appearance or at least the dominance of a new type of religious idea: dogmas.

However, we need not suppose a deep chasm between dogmatic religions and those that are mythological. A whole series of transitions allows us to go from one to the other. Within Greco-Roman polytheism, an effort is made to think about old legends and formulate a certain number of beliefs in philosophical terms, in sum, to go from images to concepts. In religions of mysteries, it is also possible to identify nascent dogmas, such as beliefs in a savior-god or in the resurrection of the initiated. Conversely, mythology remains, though the influence of myths on thinking seems to have been lost forever. Gnosticism retains the ancient Babylonian traditions; for example, its theory of redemption occurring outside of time is, according to Bousset, a cosmological narrative and in no way related to Christian dogma. Yet why search among the heresies? Does not the New Testament also contain mythical elements, particularly in Revelation? It is true that these myths play no active role in Christianity. Rather, mythology is perpetuated in the major universal religions in the stories of the founders: Jesus, Muhammad, and Buddha. Indeed, certain historians refuse to attribute historical reality to these great figures and see them as simple myths. This thesis is unacceptable (Goguel and Guignebert). However, while the founders of modern religions did in fact exist, popular imagination has been active concerning their lives.

Thus myth and dogma seem to touch for a moment. The latter, however, ends up replacing the former: it remains the only type of religious representation in civilized societies. How should it be defined?

Before it had its present meaning, the word *dogma* had two meanings among the Greeks. First, it designated the set of decisions made by civil authorities *(senatus con-sultum)* or religious leaders (Mosaic precepts, judgments of Christ). Accordingly, dogma targeted conduct and was not concerned with speculative thought. However, during the same period, philosophers gave this word another meaning: that of a summary of doctrine, in other words, a formula that condenses a teaching. Dogma, as we understand it today, is born of the union of these two meanings, of the meeting between the practical rule and the philosophical aphorism. Indeed, every dogma contains both elements:

First, dogma is imposed: it is a decision by an authority, sets the church's boundaries, and identifies heresy.

Next, dogma is an assertion of doctrine: it settles a point of faith and addresses thought.

Guignebert says, "[I]t is a theological formula that expresses the beliefs of a time and place about a point of faith and that the relevant authorities of the Church accept and impose as a rule of orthodoxy."

The history of dogmas is one of the most studied chapters of the history of ideas. However, what strikes historians are the contingencies, particularities, and chance occurrences. For them, no law can be seen in the chaos of events. One of them writes:

> The study of a dogma does not put us in the presence of a work of nature in which chance occurrences are nothing more than accidents that dominate and eliminate, with virtually no exceptions, the regular sequence of constant phenomena. It shows us a work that was produced by the human brain, in which impressions do not succeed each

> other in a set order and where contingent events are
> echoed in conclusions and decisions that are more or less
> lasting . . . to produce combinations that are sometimes
> most surprising. (Guignebert)

However, the same historian points out that dogma is "above all a social phenomenon," that it is "the expression [of faith] in a certain context," and that it "is created by the anonymous, blind co-operation" of all the faithful. Thus it belongs as much to sociology as it does to history.

Dogma is, by definition, first a social fact, since it is a rule of faith and demands submission and fidelity from the believer. Insofar as the society is characterized by constraint and the dogma is a product of a religious authority, the society and dogma will closely coincide.

It is also a social fact because it defines a community of believers. The Church created dogma each time minds were divided between extremely divergent opinions and the seamless cloth was about to be torn. Dogma is thus a rallying point and a link. Gardeil says that dogma is not a simple theological truth, but, because it has the purpose of uniting all the faithful in the same declaration of belief, it is, above all, action.

It is also a social fact in the sense that it occurs in the heart of a specific community and culture. It responds to problems that arise in that community because of that culture. Consequently, it can be understood only if it is placed back into the social and, especially, cultural context in which it developed.

Finally, it is a social fact because of its origins. "The concept of dogma is elusive. On one hand, it must be valid for all and so be popular; on the other hand, it must provide a rational formula for belief that, because of its philosophical origin, cannot be popular at all." This is to say that the meaning must be distinguished from the form. The form is invented by the theologian responsible for translating the often confused and contradictory sentiments of the masses into a clean formula. However, the subject matter is provided by the masses. Dogma is not handed down from on high. Otherwise it would be difficult to understand how it could be imposed so easily. It expresses the aspirations and nostalgia of the group of the faithful. It springs up from below. It is "the work of living, anonymous faith." Certainly, theological speculation can be the remote preparation for the establishment of dogmas. That of the Immaculate Conception, for example, is the conclusion of a highly refined deduction. However, this activity of the learned is insufficient: "The environment determines the real influence that individuals can have" (Guignebert).

This is where we encounter the limits of sociology. Faith, even when it is collective, is not a simple social fact or a mere reflection of the structure of the city or the nation. It has its own existence. Its development is the result of deepened spiritual life, which is internal work. Thus the history of dogmas is at the crossroads of two series of laws: those of mystical life and those of sociology.

There are two ways to think about the evolution of dogma. The first is that of Renan. A dogma that develops changes its meaning. Catholicism is mistaken in its claim that its dogmas do not change. New beliefs are born, such as that of the infallibility of the pope, and there are beliefs, if not dogma, that die, such as that of the end of the world in the year 1000. What does not change is the formulation. However, while the words may stay the same, different ideas are understood. How could it be otherwise? The work of codification carries the marks of a specific period and milieu, and, in consequence, "historically... dogma cannot remain immobile except by condemning itself to ruin."

On the contrary, the orthodox view is that dogma develops as an organic growth. All later complications and all the present doctrinal luxuriance were included and implied in the first formulations of the nascent Church. The synods and the popes simply brought out new elements that had been virtually enclosed in the traditional theological premises.

We think that these two conceptions are not mutually exclusive. They shed light on certain laws of the birth of dogmas: one on sociological laws, the other on laws that might be called religious. The latter reveal to us the persevering work of faith on itself, while the former show the necessity that faith be incarnated in a historically and geographically defined humanity.

This said, is seems possible to analyze the work of historians to find a certain number of laws that express something about this dual evolution. The laws we borrow are from historians of Christianity, but they seem valid in general for Islam and Buddhism.

First, the passage from the negative to the positive. Dogmas are born out of heresies. They are the result of a long series of discussions in which the fate of the Church seems to be in question. Despite their positive formulations, they are more condemnations of opinions than they are affirmations. For example, the dual nature of Christ was proclaimed against those who wanted to recognize only his divine nature and who took his human nature as pure appearance. However, faith quickly views the dogma in a positive manner, reflects on its foundations, and creates a theology.

Second, the law of extension. Faith tends to unceasingly extend divinity. The pope, a simple bishop of Rome subject to the synods with only an honorary preeminence, ended up obtaining, in 1870, infallible mastery of the faith. Christ was first a god with a miraculous birth, but the Virgin is subject to the same condition, and a long process of extension was required to result in the dogma of the Virgin conceived without sin.

Third, the law of complication. The first dogmas are relatively simple formulas with their source in the need to think of religious emotion in contemporary philosophical terms. However, philosophy is rich, diverse, and, above all, changing, which explains the subsequent need to reconcile formulations that are sometimes contradictory, at least in appearance. This is the beginning of many complications, of which the history of the dogma of the Trinity is an excellent illustration.

CHAPTER 4

Prohibitions
Relations between Religion and Morality

Even the most philosophical religious representations, such as dogmas, are never pure representations. They are experienced as much as they are thought and raise a whole world of feelings, fears, and fervor within the soul. They lead to action or prevent it and culminate in obligations or prohibitions.

We customarily call prohibitions "taboos." Though the word is Polynesian, the fact is very general and can be found under different names among all peoples: the Malaysian *pamali*, the Indian *wakan*, the Fan *eki*, the Madagascan *fady*, the Bantu *mzio*, and so on. Of course, the meaning of all these words is not exactly the same. Their significations are more or less broad. *Fady*, for example, has a much wider meaning than the Polynesian *tabu* and includes a large number of prohibitive superstitions of which the sacred nature, if there was one, has greatly diminished. However, these details are of little importance.

A taboo always acts as a brake: do not perform that action, do not eat that food, do not touch that object. Initially, this is what is striking about it. A prohibition supposes a prior conception of what is sacred or impure and entails a whole series of consequences for the person who violates it, such as death and disease. The definition of *taboo* must take into account these positive elements along with the negative rule by which it is expressed. Thus we shall say, in agreement with the author of the article in the *Encyclopaedia Britannica*, that taboo includes three elements: recognition of the sacred or impure nature of a given person or thing, the prohibition that follows from this recognition, and the punishment entailed by violation of this prohibition.

We can distinguish the following:

General taboos, which apply to an entire class of individuals (those belonging to the kangaroo clan may neither kill nor eat kangaroos), must be distinguished from specific taboos, which apply only to certain individuals in a class.

Permanent taboos, which cannot be lifted (such as in the case of the ancient Mikado, who could not touch the ground), must be distinguished from provisory taboos, which are in effect only for a period, for example, so long as an island is taboo, no canoe may land there, but once the danger of mystical contagion has passed, the taboo is lifted.

Common taboos, which require abstention from a number of activities but nonetheless allow a large degree of freedom, must be distinguished from strict taboos, which rule out the whole activity: all fire is put out, all canoes are pulled out of the river, and all members of the community are prohibited from coming out of their huts, bathing, and cutting their hair. A vast web of prohibitions traps indigenous people in its subtle threads.

Taboos of privilege, which result from the sacred nature of persons or objects and their eminent saintliness and isolate chiefs, priests, and temples, must be distinguished from taboos of disqualification, which result, on the contrary, from the impurity of beings and objects and isolate, for example, the sick, the dead, and the wounded.

Direct taboos, which we have just described and are the most important, must be distinguished from indirect or transmitted taboos, which result from the contagious nature of saintliness or impurity. Among some peoples, if a chief blows on the fire, the fire also becomes taboo and can no longer be used to cook food.

The sanctions that follow the violation of these taboos may be either mystical or legal. Lévy-Bruhl has focused mainly on "mystical" sanctions. Every accident or unfortunate incident reveals a wrongdoing. Most indigenous people believe that beings and objects take revenge all by themselves and that wrongdoing is a mechanical cause of punishment, sickness, or death. However, a violation does not affect the individual alone: it can also be serious for the society. If a disastrous storm occurs, it is because a young woman, for example, combed her hair outside the house. The chief's mission is thus to make sure taboos are observed, since compliance with them safeguards the happiness of the community. This is how legal and civil sanctions come to be added to mystical ones: the death sentence in Hawaii, confiscated goods in Fiji, or the fine of a bull among the Bara. By passing into the hands of a chief, the taboo becomes an instrument of government and is used to increase the leader's power.

Taboos have been used not only to reinforce the power of chiefs. According to Freud, Le Roy, Reinach, and Van Gennep, they have also had other uses. They have protected the weak, such as women, children, and servants, from the mischief of the strong. While their origin is not prophylactic, taboos have been used for hygiene by requiring that corpses be isolated. They have regulated major natural processes and established discipline where instinctive violence could bring about only disorder, in particular during pregnancy. Many matrimonial taboos have provided effective protection for the fetus during its development. Some have protected incipient property from theft.

Yet, while taboos really have had these consequences, they have also had a morally edifying effect on primitive animal barbarism, and we might therefore be inclined to see them as the first form of moral commandment. This is Jevons's thesis.

This confusion was caused by the fact that taboos appear in the form of categorical imperatives. They are, according to Reinach, "unjustified prohibitions." From this point of view, taboos are similar to moral duties that, according to Kant, prohibit or command unconditionally: "Moral action is necessary in itself and unrelated to any other end. It is an objective necessity."

Marillier has tried to eliminate this confusion. He notes that, while taboos are indeed absolute obligations, this is an attribute shared by all social customs. Customs of communities are, like those of individuals, all the stronger when they are unreasoned reflexes. The first taboos were justified. There were religious reasons for them; they may appear strange to us today, but they were reasons just the same. Taboos then proliferated and became consolidated in customs, and their original reasons were gradually forgotten. Thus taboos went from hypothetical imperatives to categorical imperatives, but it can be seen that this is true "insofar as they are customary, and to that degree only. They are so in the same way and for the same reasons as other customs."

Thus taboos, no matter what their obligatory nature, have nothing to do with moral duty. It has even been possible to argue just as aptly for the opposite thesis and to denounce such ritual prohibitions as a terrible instrument of social stagnation.

This is claimed, for example, by Richard in his book, *Évolution des moeurs*. Carefully thought-out awareness of moral laws, the feeling of personal dignity, and a concern for justice could have emerged only on the condition that the ancient conception of physical purity was eliminated. Peter says: "You yourselves know how unlawful it is for a Jew to associate with or to visit any one of another nation; but God has shown me that I should not call any man common or unclean" (Acts 10:28). The most formidable obstacle faced by the Greek moralists in their reform was superstition, which Theophrastes considered to be characterized mainly by taboo-driven scruples. Thus morals progressed by eliminating taboos, just as medicine progressed by eliminating the idea of possession.

When taboo triumphs, it is to the detriment of morals. For example, ritual anthropophagy is found mainly among peoples with the most numerous and restrictive religious prohibitions. Anthropophagy requires war as its natural complement, since the people killed and eaten in sacred ceremonies are chosen from among prisoners of war. Hospitality, on the contrary, has permitted the development of human cooperation, which is the only possible foundation for progress. Cooperation could have been born only on the ruins of the idea of taboo. Strangers are intrinsically impure, and only a weakening of the belief in the contagious power of impurity opens the way to extending moral relations.

Generally, while disciplining the instincts is necessary, so is free expression of legitimate tendencies. As they multiply, taboos tighten the human pupa in a casing too rigid to allow it to escape.

If taboos were always rigid, life would be impossible. However, life knows how to build roads and avoid obstacles. So, to free itself, it creates rituals in which prohibitions are lifted. The harmful influence is removed by being cast onto a powerful being that can withstand it with impunity. By bathing or splashing oneself, the evil is transmitted to the river, which carries it away. By passing through the trees and rocks, it is caught on bumps of stone or rough bark. Above all, there are times when taboos are lifted: a great chief may eliminate those previously proclaimed by subordinates or abolish his own. Finally, we have seen that many taboos are only temporary: things that were prohibited at one time return later as common practices.

These fissures allow creative action to emerge.

There are quite a number of explanations of taboos. The most well known is the contagionist theory, which is argued for by English ethnologists, the Durkheimian school, and independent theorists such as Van Gennep. Smith showed the ambiguity of the notion of sacred. A sacred object both elicits respect and terrifies. It gives rise to both love and fear. The ideas of impurity and holiness can be separated later, but they always share the same sphere, and taboos are signs of their contiguity. Thus, menstrual blood is taboo because it is impure, yet it is also full of magical power. People and things are thus charged with impurity and holiness, as "a Leyden jar is charged with accumulated electricity and, just as the electricity can be discharged through contact with a good conductor, saintliness or virtue can also be discharged" (Frazer). This entails two dangers: danger for the sacred being, because it could lose its mystical power and be emptied of its occult strength, and also danger for the profane being, for what is taboo cannot be approached with impunity. The most minor contact with it leads to destruction, and imprudence is punished by death, disease, and misfortune.

This theory crushed the previous animist theory, which claimed that taboos arose out of a fear of spirits. However, it did not eliminate the animist theory altogether, which has today, after a period of dormancy, suddenly reappeared.

A third theory is that of the partisans of primitive monotheism. When referring to noncivilized societies, Le Roy prefers to use the Bantus and the Pygmies as examples because of the extremely archaic nature of their civilizations. According to them, the Master of Things reserves his share of nature's resources and uses poisoning, disease, and floods to establish what is his and punish those who are tempted to claim part of the wealth. Thus natural resources must be used carefully. There are some things that should not be done. The existence of taboos requires, in consequence, prior belief in a god who is the master of things because he is their creator.

Psychoanalysis proposes a fourth theory. Some people who are mentally ill surround themselves with prohibitions. They forbid themselves to do certain things or use certain words that they claim are dangerous for them. Freud goes on from there. He notes that the analogy between taboos and obsession is probably external and related more to symptoms than to an identity in kind. Yet he points out suggestive similarities. Obsessions and taboos are both absurd and unjustified. In both cases the most frequent prohibition is contact. Both are defenses against what could be contagious and transmissible. In the case of one of Freud's patients, everything that reminded him of Mrs. Cerf became taboo, for example an object bought on Cerf Street. Both can also be eliminated through special ceremonies: there is a strict parallel between obsessive ablution and noncivilized purification. However, the origin of this psychosis must be found in the (sexual) pleasure of touch and the social prohibition of such contact. It is this dual character of being pleasant and prohibited, the oscillation of the sick mind between these two opposing feelings, that explains the "ambiguity" of the obsessive taboo. Here there is also no justification because the primitive reason determining the prohibition has been repressed in the unconscious, and morbid taboos are contagious because desire tends to be transferred onto another object in order to escape social censure. Why, therefore, could not the taboos of noncivilized peoples also result from the repression of burning desires?

We readily recognize that Freud is careful to oppose the altruism of the patient who fears for his loved ones to the egoism of the savage who fears only for himself. Thus he does not go so far as identification: "Taboo is not a neurosis but a product of society." However, he tends to see in neurosis a sort of idea of taboo since he summarizes his thesis in the following way: "It could almost be said that hysteria is an imperfect work of art, obsessive neurosis a deformed religion, and paranoia a warped philosophical system." However, this greatly reduces the importance of the psychoanalytic thesis. It throws indirect light on taboo, but does not explain it.

The three preceding religious theses remain. While they may be in opposition, they seem to us to be equally justified. This is because taboo, as Foucart saw very well, is a complex notion that "brings together a certain number of unrelated facts . . . [and] . . . cannot be reduced to a single principle, no matter how simple." Certain taboos result from the contagious nature of the sacred, others from the fear of spirits, and others from belief in a god who is master of all things. What must be said, however, is that, contrary to the views of the contagionist school, animist taboos are much more numerous than was thought only a few years ago. Menstrual blood, for example, is not harmful in itself, but because it harbors a terrible Spirit, analogous to that of a fetus born prematurely (Lévy-Bruhl).

When we go from tribal religions to the major religions, prohibitions do not disappear. Instead, they take on a new form: that of sin.

> The idea of sin is not presented in the same way... in the various religious doctrines.... In Chinese thought... an infraction is seen as an action contrary to "nature" that shortens one's life, or as a failure to remember the Tao.... Hindu doctrine conceives of an infraction as a rupture in equilibrium caused by an individual assertion contrary to the Dharma, the law of being.... In Islam, sin appears as a revolt and negation.... The Christian conception is closely related to the theory of Adam's fall.... Sin is envisaged under all aspects of the temptation and fall, in other words, under all the Luciferian, satanic aspects of the symbolism of woman. (Schuon)

In taboos, sanctions are analytically linked to infractions, while in sin, the relation tends to be synthetic. As soon as a taboo is violated, the sacred powers or demons are set into action. Sin, in contrast, is disobedience of an order given by a personal divinity. Under the law of taboos, intent does not count: whether or not it is voluntary, the crime automatically sets off the evil powers. Human will plays a role in sin: a contract is broken, so God withdraws his divine mercy and benevolence. The faithful are punished, but they are punished because God wills it. The punishment is related to the crime only synthetically. It is possible for it to not occur, in which case grace would be granted. However, since the sinner was the one who broke the contract, that person has a responsibility, which is initially shared and extends to the whole group as well as to later generations: "The fathers ate un-ripe grapes and their children's teeth were set on edge be-cause of it." It is individualized later.

Thus, in the idea of punishment a transformation oc-curs that can be correlated with that occurring when taboo becomes sin.

Violating a taboo results in immediate punishment. There is no need to wait to see the fatal consequences. However, in the case of sin, since the relation uniting the punishment and the crime is synthetic and depends on the will of the outraged god, punishment may be delayed. Often it occurs in this world and strikes those who are truly guilty. In Judea, Mesopotamia, and Mexico, it often fell only on the son, allowing the father to enjoy the fruits of his crimes. Finally, it may occur only in the great shad-owy world of the beyond.

Therefore, we must now say a word about primitive representations of life beyond the grave. Marillier, who has conducted an extensive study of this among savage people, notes that, among them, myths do not use moral-ity as a scale to determine the fate of souls after death. The beyond is generally the more or less faded copy of the land of the living, and spirits there have a washed-out, feeble existence (Australia, New Guinea, Madagascar). However, the fate of the dead may vary. The differences in their destinies are not the results of differences in moral-ity, but of social distinctions: kings, chiefs, and priests have special places. Elsewhere the difference has to do instead with the nature of the death: in Mexico, the warrior who died on the battlefield, the prisoner who was sacrificed, and the woman who died in childbirth each went to a special realm. Another frequent idea is that death is a kind of initiation with a series of tests. Only powerful souls or those with knowledge of magical secrets manage to triumph over the numerous obstacles and arrive in the land of the blessed. Among the Huron, the dead must ride across a shadowy river on a log while being savagely attacked by a dog.

Little by little, however, moral influences are introduced into these ideas. Steinmetz observed, against Marillier, that these myths are not entirely free of morality, because the social hierarchy is often popularly thought to correspond to a moral hierarchy and so the special fate reserved for chiefs is already a sort of reward for virtue. When the condition of the shadows also depends on the nature of the death, is courage not considered meritorious? Finally, among some peoples, piety was as effective as skill in magic in overcoming the challenges that the spirits of the dead encountered along the way. Despite everything, these are only sketches attesting to the beginnings of a concern for morality. Ethical concerns have not yet transformed the mythical representations of the beyond.

How does this transformation occur? Initially, punishment of the guilty is only a vendetta continued in the other world. At Motlaw, murderers and adulterers found their victims barring their way into heaven. At Aurora, the victims attacked those who had harmed them. Then, as the authority of the gods increases, they become judges and punish sacrilege first and then crimes against others, such as moral failings.

History confirms this finding. In Egypt, the entrance of the dead into paradise was the result of magical operations. It was only very late that the judgment of souls and the confession of sins were introduced into this eschatology. In Homer's Greece, corpses led a reduced existence in the beyond, but an existence that was a continuation of the one in life. While there is a tribunal of the dead in the Odyssey, it is only because judges kept the jobs they had on Earth. Tantale and Tityos punished sacrilege, not sin. It was not until Pindar that there arose the idea that tarnished souls paid for their crimes after death. In Vedic India, the belief in judgment in the beyond did not appear clearly; indeed it never appeared completely, because the theory of metapsychology grew considerably. However, metapsychology took on an ethical character. The study of the Jewish idea of Sheol led to analogous conclusions.

Throughout this chapter, we have gathered the materials we need to achieve an overall view of the relations between morality and religion.

Few issues have been so controversial. I will leave aside those who continue the thought of Constant, who distinguish, with Tiele and Sabatier, morality from religion but consider both to derive from a nebulous primitive feeling of human impotence, because, as has already been noted, the origin of this feeling is recent.

Partisans of the union between morality and religion have been recruited from the most diametrically opposed schools. Some are Catholic, such as Lagrange, Le Roy, and Schmidt. They believe in primitive revelation. According to them, the most backward peoples, such as the Pygmies and the Fuegians, are precisely those who have the purest morality. Later, magic causes these initial virtues to disappear and makes bloodthirsty instincts and hatreds rise up from the bestiality that is within the human heart. The secret societies of warlocks would be the schools of these instincts. However, while religion can be distinguished from magic, morality is always the consequence of religious life. According to Wundt, "All moral imperatives are originally like religious commandments." Caird states, "In their initial periods, religion and morality are necessarily correlated."

However, the most ardent proponents of the thesis we are analyzing are sociologists of the French school. They note first that when we compare the religious rules of primitive people with present moral obligations, they seem to have nothing in common. However, a confusion slips into this way of seeing things: that of our morality with absolute morality. That the gods of the semicivilized are responsible for the strangest prescriptions does not mean that religion is independent of morality but that the concepts these people have of good and bad are not the same as our own.

In the end, morality is nothing but the set of rules that governs social cooperation. Does not religion produce this very community of people by centering it on their gods? The essential point of Durkheim's thesis is that religion is the experienced feeling of social solidarity and gods are never anything more than hypostases of the collective mind. This would mean that religion is responsible for maintaining cohesion among people.

They note, second, that all features of morality have their sources in religiousness. The dualism of good and bad follows from the dualism of the sacred and the profane worlds. Moral imperatives are extensions of taboos, which also command categorically. It is true that religion imposes beliefs and a morality of action, but, aside from the fact that this difference applies more to present-day churches than to primitive cults, this distinction arbitrarily divides what is naturally united. Thoughts and actions always overlap to some degree. Society does not merely give orders. It is also the object of love, and the gods who symbolize it are not only feared for their prohibitions; they are fervently worshiped. They set a certain number of ideals above physical life, and humanity strives to attain them.

We can subscribe to the first argument of the French school of sociology: we ourselves should also avoid all confusion. However, while this argument clears the field, it proves nothing in itself. The second argument is not decisive, either. It assigns religion the task of maintaining social cohesion at the same time that it makes religious feeling the experience of such cohesion. We can agree that religion strengthens social relationships. However, we must agree with Bergson that "when we say that one of the purposes of religion, as it was designed by nature, is to maintain social life, we do not mean that there is solidarity between the religion and morality." One may help the other even if they are independent of each other. In particular, as Belot writes, "for society to feel its own unity in the form of the community of religious belief, this community must exist prior to it, at least to some degree." Most gods are deifications of natural phenomena, especially of stars, and can therefore express the community only indirectly. It seems there is no god that is a direct hypostasis of society. This is because among primitive people the social meaning is instinctive, never thought out and even less deified. Perceptions can be deified, not unconscious tendencies.

Moral laws, like religious rules, compel. However, we have seen with Marillier why taboos constrain: they are social customs that are inherited from the past and place the full weight of tradition on the shoulders of new generations. Insofar as moral rules are customs, they prescribe in the same manner. However, these two forms of rules resemble each other only indirectly, not because of some identity of nature. On the contrary, it is said that Marillier liked to cite the case of the taboo in certain Indian tribes that required women to give birth outside of the village and the husband who, as he carried his wife out to a big hole full of ice so that she could give birth to their child, cried profusely because he feared she would not be able to withstand the harsh torture of the cold. Here morality challenges the authority of religious customs. Morality is, in effect, the appearance of new values, and in order for these values to triumph, they must first eliminate the conformism required by formalist religions.

This is why many thinkers, such as Tylor, Guyau, Le Bon, Belot, Westermarck, and Bouglé, see morality as resulting from social needs:

> It seems to be a constant that no purely moral nature or function is intrinsic to primitive gods.... The obligations people have to each other differ deeply from those they have to the gods.... Gods are probably called in later to guarantee oaths and contracts.... But when they are called in to sanction rules, in a sense those rules preexist the gods. What makes this even more striking is that even as

they are invoked as guarantors of morality, they are not
subject to it themselves, and their immorality... is not
shocking since they are not expected to be models. (Belot)

All we can retain from Durkheim's thesis is that religion, which originally colored virtually all activities, also
colors moral activity. However, color does not mean identity. Let us listen to Belot on this point once again:

If history is simply the description of appearances and the
order in which they occur, we could say that, historically,
everything springs from religion. However, in this sense
the idea of origin is confused and ambiguous, entirely
unlike a scientific explanation. To confuse them would be
to commit an enormous *cum hoc, ergo propter hoc.*

Further on he says:

If at some point morality and law win their independence from religion, it is because, in spite of everything, a
minimum of social relations were directly governed by
a certain real propriety and were in no way determined
by religious beliefs. It is this secular activity that, by
developing and becoming organized, produced morality,
and this cracked its religious wrappings. To say that
religion produced morality is to confuse the shell with
the seed.

Two remarks need to be made. While from the most
ancient times religion has been, at least theoretically, independent of morality, it is still useful to it as a technique
for educating the will. By teaching people to pull away
from themselves, control their material interests, and con-
quer their passions, it teaches sacrifice and self-abnegation.
However, such education is gradual, and very often orgias-

tic religions, far from teaching self-control, have let loose the worst madness.

Morality and religion are united in the major ethical religions, such as Buddhism and Christianity. It has been said that this union was the greatest revolution in history. Now, in addition to independent morality, which cannot *not* exist since it necessarily results from life in society, religious morality has appeared. Certainly the latter can be a regression: "Certain sects...have claimed that the saints could do anything. Others...that purification ceremonies could erase any trace of sin" (Goblet d'Alviella). However, the advantages of this union outweigh the evil it can cause. The great moral upheavals occurred in the shadows of the churches. Nonconformists, who portend new times, take their strength from the power of faith. Beyond the rigid ethics of the priest there is, to use the Bergsonian expression, the "open morality" of the prophet and the inspired.

CHAPTER 5

Driving Elements
Rituals

While today religion is essentially a system of beliefs, it was first a set of rituals. However, just as myths extend beyond religion, through the explanations they give of natural phenomena or the poetry involved, some rituals are exclusively social. These can be found in the West, for example in diplomatic protocol or major secular celebrations. However, they are especially evident in the East: Confucian ceremonies are purely civil and have no religious features. At least, this was the opinion of the Jesuits, who did not fear participating in them. We will not discuss ritualism except insofar as it refers to sacred matters or beings. Both are fearsome and inspire dread. However, they are also helpful powers and useful to possess, which naturally explains the desire not to flee, but to acquire them. Nevertheless, they must be used with care, and one must calculate one's actions and weigh one's words. Thus is born the "sacred action" (Loisy), which initially takes on a ritual character.

Just as we never find isolated themes, only thematic sequences, we generally find only ceremonial sequences. We will look at two examples: sequences of sacrifice and of initiation, one from the work of Hubert and Mauss and one from that of Van Gennep.

The outline of sacrifice is consecration of the initiator of the sacrifice, sacrificer, place, and instruments; consecration and destruction of the victim; and then exit rites.

The outline for rites of passage is separation rites; liminal rites, which govern the period of transition; and then rites of incorporation.

The latter sequence appears to span a considerable number of rituals. Indeed, could not all religious rites be included in it? Do they not always consist in an initial separation from profane life, followed by an incorporation into the divine world? This chapter will therefore distinguish preliminary rites, which prepare people for the passage and mystical transformation, from rites of union.

Preliminary Rites

The sacred cannot be approached unless one is free of all contamination. This is the reason for an initial series of rites: purification rites, which can be celebrated in isolation, but are generally used as a prelude to all religious, and even all magical, ceremonies.

Three concepts interlace. First, there is that of elimination; evil is considered to be a power that has penetrated into individuals independently of their will and that must be expelled. If evil and the individuals are now one and the same, if the beings are so contaminated that even their most minute fibers are affected, elimination becomes purification. Finally, when impure persons wish to reject their sins in order to calm the irritated god and when a nostalgia for regenerative suffering arises from within them, then purification will be transformed into expiation.

Sacramental purification is performed using the most varied procedures, of which bathing is the most well known. According to Wundt, it must have been borrowed from the ancient belief in the magical powers of springs and rivers that, because they are used to quench the thirst of animals and grow plants, drain mana off into their waters. When this is added to the observation that certain thermal springs can heal ailments, the purifying power of water is acknowledged. Ceremonial washing has a long history. While many religions have given way to many others, it always survives. It can even be seen in Christian baptism, but, of course, a revolution has occurred in the religious representations relating to the rite. The water no longer acts directly through its own magical power. Instead, the priest of the church invests the water with the Holy Spirit, which alone has regenerative power.

Fire and blood can also be used for purification. One of the most widespread procedures is to transfer the evil or malevolent power to an object or animal that is then destroyed. Frazer's *Scapegoat* is an important monograph on this subject. Just as one can transfer a load of wood or stones to someone else, it is possible to hand over one's sins or illness. Sometimes evil is personified as a devil (represented by a person), who is driven out with sticks (California, Queensland, and Cambodia), and sometimes the malevolent power remains invisible and people imagine that it resides in a material object that must take it far away, such as a little boat set afloat on a river or on the sea (Malaysian peninsula), a consecrated animal (cow, goat, or chicken), or a wanderer or prisoner (Nigeria and Siam).

We can leave aside other procedures, such as beating the air, consumption of certain plants (laurel leaves in the case of the Greeks), fumigation, and ventilation, to turn to oral rituals.

Revelation of fault is a means of purification for primitives because, as Lévy-Bruhl tells us, the stain of a sin that remains secret grows, but when it is confessed, its spread is stemmed. On Rossell Island, difficult deliveries occur when the woman has committed adultery, but if she reveals the name of her accomplice, the child is born easily. The sin leaves with the words that are pronounced: it is expelled from the heart through the mouth. The evolution of the practice can be followed in the case of the Semites by comparing the penitential psalms of the Assyro-Babylonians with those of the Hebrews. From the former to the latter, the magical process of elimination of evil through speech was transformed into magnificent prayers of faith in God. Confession is one of the rare procedures of purification that has survived in the major universal religions because it was particularly easy to give it a spiritual and moral meaning. It is found in Mithraism, in Buddhism, of which it is one of the rare ceremonies, and in Christianity.

Purification makes people fit to approach the gods and opens the way to sacrifice. However, it must first be known whether the sacrifice will be effective, whether it will be welcomed by the gods or scorned. This explains the need for divination.

The major problem here is to determine whether divination is related to magic or to religion. For Bouché-Leclerc, Davies, Henry, and Doutté, magic and divination are related through their shared origins and officiants. However, while these authors agree on the principle, they are divided with respect to its application. Davies, for example, finds the roots of divination in demonology. He considers it to be a case of asking spirits to reveal the future. Doutté considers it to come from sympathetic magic: the barn owl, for example, is unlucky and also an ill omen, for the prediction is nothing but the continuation of an initial unpleasant impression. It is a fear before it becomes a prediction. Frazer, Hubert, and Mauss take the opposite tack and locate divination completely outside of magic.

Actually, in this case as in the case of taboo, the unity of the goal hides a great complexity of origins. The processes of divination reveal a wide range of cultural practices. The desired goal is all that links them and brings them together as a whole (Foucart). Thus crystallomancy is pure magic; astrology is based on pseudoscientific observations; ornithomancy assumes a belief in the sacred value of birds, which is the remains of ancient animal worship; necromancy follows from ancestor worship; and divination by entrails presupposes sacrifice. The future is imagined to be contained in the viscera of victims, according to Loisy, because it was initially thought that a given species of animal had a mystical relation with a human group (totemism) and carried in it the destiny of that group. In order to have foreknowledge of that destiny, was it not necessary to kill the animal and examine its entrails? The various techniques employed by divination are thus borrowed from both magic and religion.

However, if this mystical origin is accepted, we must admit that as divination becomes more complicated it increasingly tends to look like a pseudoscience. First, with respect to its procedures, for it uses observation and reasoning. It employs observation when it notes the influence of the moon on vegetation and of climate on people's characters. It uses reasoning when it concludes that the carnivorous crow that eats corpses comes to know the animals whose bodies it eats, including the future that is written in their entrails. Next, with respect to its principle, it supposes a belief in determinism, the idea of rigid laws. In Chaldea, especially, divination took on this scientific character, which simply became more distinct as time went on.

Divinatory rites seem to be among the most primitive. They are based on an instinctive human tendency to want to know what the future holds. For the same reason, despite ecclesiastical prohibitions and harsh repression, they continue today, even in Christianity, for example in the form of dreams sent by God, apocalyptic visions, and spells taken from holy writings.

These rites are extremely complicated. However, they can be divided into two groups that seem to exist simultaneously, with only their order of appearance differing depending on the people. There is inductive divination, which goes from the sign to the thing that is signified; for example, the direction of the flight of a bird announces good or bad fortune. Then there is intuitive divination, which operates through the intermediary of visionaries and necromancers and does not proceed from the extraordinary event to its meaning, but by listening to divine internal or external voices.

When forms of divination are compared, a few vague laws are revealed.

First, there is the law of localization. Initially, all phenomena can be omens and it is up to the seers to recognize them. However, the field of revelations ends up restricted to a few types of events that are determined in accordance with the culture. In order for birds to predict the future, their flight must be within the sacred space. Of course, localization is never complete, and in addition to consecrated signs there are always chance events (Bouché-Leclerc).

Second, there is the law of linkage. Contrary to most rites, which can exist independently of the representations that gave rise to them and can be given new interpretations, divinatory practices remain forever linked to a system of thought. Thus, ornithomancy disappears when the city develops sacrifice and places the greatest importance on divination by entrails, but comes back into honor again with Pythagoreanism (Hubert and Mauss).

Rites of Union: Sacrifice

We will begin with Loisy's definition of sacrifice, which is broad enough to encompass all cases: "Sacrifice is a ritual action, i.e., the destruction of a sentient object that is alive or supposed to contain life, in exchange for which the invisible forces are supposed to be influenced, either to spare the sacrificers from their attacks ... or to ... provide them with satisfaction and tribute and enter into communication or even communion with them." Thus sacrifice is not a particular species of rite, but a kind that contains many. The Germans distinguish thanking sacrifice *(Dankopfer)*, requesting sacrifice *(Bittopfer)*, and collective and individual expiatory sacrifice *(Sühn* and *Sündopfer)*. One's theory of sacrifice will depend on which one is considered most primitive.

Tylor's theory portrays sacrifice as originally a self-interested gift to the spirits: *do ut des*. When the spirits left the bush or the forest to ascend to the sky and become gods, the motivated gift was replaced by homage without any hope of return. Finally, later, sentiments were presented to the gods instead of tangible objects: sacrifice became renunciation.

This theory was generally accepted until Smith replaced it with that of the anteriority of communion sacrifice in his book, *The Religion of the Semites* (1889).

According to his theory, sacrifice cannot initially be a gift because offering presupposes two feelings: that of personal property and that of duties to the gods. These feelings are not primitive, and our nomadic ancestors could not have had them because they require being tied to the land and the advent of a religious feeling devoid of any magic. It is likely that sacrifice is older than individual property, older than the time when the owner of a cow or camel had the right to part with it. Moreover, for sacrifice to become a gift, the object sacrificed cannot have a religious nature; the animal victim has to be only an animal, which presupposes a time when the ideas of taboo and the sacred have already lost their power.

Sacrifice is different from a pious offering. It is a meal. The Hebrew gods, like the gods of Homer, ate the smoke of meat. The alimentary nature is very clear when drink is offered because as it is absorbed into the ground it appears to be consumed by underground gods. However, in addition to sacrifices in which everything seems to be devoured by the gods, there are others in which the gods make do with part of the victim, such as the fat or blood, and the rest is eaten by people. By eating the same food, communion between the faithful and the gods is achieved. Smith, who considers totemism to be the religion of the most backward people, such as the Australians, claims to prove that this is the primitive form of the rite by describing the communal totemic sacrifice of a white camel by nomadic Bedouins.

Sacrifice still exists in Catholicism. What is the Mass but, through the bread and wine, the absorption of the community's God through the priest, who is the community's representative? However, while it may still exist, it is nonetheless the oldest form of sacrifice, that from which all the others are derived. Expiatory sacrifice in periods of distress, when the god seems to be withdrawing protection from the people, is communion with that god to bring the defense back. Sacrificial gifts appear only after royalty is established and result from the union of religious beliefs with the initially secular practice of tithes or royal taxes. Sacrifice then takes on the appearance of a tribute paid to God, the belated product of religious evolution, since it clearly supposes the concept of a god-king modeled after an earthly king.

Not only have the various forms of sacrifice developed beyond their origins in primitive communion; communion sacrifice has also evolved. Originally, the sacred animal that was killed and eaten was the ancestor of the clan: the totem. However, totemism exists only among people who have not yet reached the stage of animal husbandry. When the pastoral system is established, a second category of animal appears, which is not sacred in itself.

Therefore, before such animals are sacrificed, preliminary consecrating rituals must be performed to render them divine. Human sacrifice, which was once believed to be primitive because of its barbarism, instead comes later. It supposes the idea of the gift, and human life is the most precious gift of all. The progress of civilization eliminates this aberrant form.

These are Smith's main ideas. They are based on data borrowed from the Semites alone, but they were confirmed by facts in a striking manner, for totemic communion, which was intuited rather than actually observed by Smith, was suddenly discovered in Australia. It takes the form of the Intichiuma, a ceremony that finishes with a banquet at which the members of the clan consume their own totem together.

Frazer developed an original thesis by taking Smith's research and uniting it with Mannhardt's studies on agrarian demons. According to this thesis, primitive people do not conceive of the idea of eternity. Gods are stronger than people, but they die just the same. Even the Greeks had tombs for Zeus and Dionysus. Since the course of nature is dependent on the existence of these man-gods, their decrepitude is the sign of death for plants and the animals in the fields. Since old age is inevitable, there is only one way to avoid the danger: the god must be killed and the divine power transferred into a younger body. In Mexico, for example, the aboriginal people chose one of their prisoners, worshiped him as a god for six months and then killed, skinned, and ate him. They then dressed a new prisoner in his skin so as to represent the new god.

At the same time, the former god who had been sacrificed took with him sickness and sin, thus playing the role of the scapegoat.

Mannhardt showed that May Roses, Green Georges, and carnivals symbolize the spirit of plants. Often a pretense is made of killing them, and these ritual simulations are the vestiges of ancient murders. The cults of Attis, Osiris, and Demeter, with their myths of death and resurrection, prove how ancient such sacrifice is. Yet they are still nothing more than transformations of simpler rites, in which people killed and ate the spirit of wheat, barley, or rice in the form of a human (a stranger rolled into the last sheaf) or an animal (a wolf, dog, or hare). Thus ritual murder is related to totemism.

We can criticize Smith for basing his theory on too narrow a foundation: the immolation of a white camel by nomadic Arabs in the fourth century A.D. As Foucart notes, there is nothing similar in the Chaldean and Egyptian rituals of the fourth century B.C. It is curious that people of 400 A.D. could have had better access to the true meaning of sacrifice than our more distant ancestors! It is true that Smith's foundation was extended with the discovery of the Intichiuma. However, even if the general and primitive natures of totemism were proven, which they are not, it remains that the Intichiuma is not limited to a banquet but includes offerings to the totem that is to be sacrificed, and in consequence, the offering does not appear later than the communion. Moreover, Smith's argument concerning the late development of private property is also not convincing, since gaining a god's favor by offering food and drink has nothing to do with the property system. The thesis we are examining probably begins with a real fact, which is that people often eat part of the sacrifice. However, as Oldenberg says, they do not do so in order to commune with the god but because, by absorbing the food that the god has tasted, they incorporate a little of the mystical power that has entered it. Finally, expiatory sacrifice appears at the same time as alimentary communion, and it is difficult to make the latter the source of the former. If the victim were impregnated with sin and evil, how could it be eaten? It would pass on part of its impurity, and expiation could never emerge from communion.

Agrarian sacrifices are also not primitive: the sacrifice *of* a god could have developed only after sacrifice *to* a god. By becoming impregnated with mystical virtues through rituals of consecration, the victim gradually becomes divine. However, at no time does the god truly transfer into the victim: the god and the victim are not identical. The proof of this can be seen in the Aztec ritual on which Frazer placed such importance: the prisoner to be killed becomes a god only through a series of imitative rites, and thus by a prior consecration.

We are thus led to new theories. Grant Allen's euhemerism sees the origin of sacrifice, like the rest of religion, in ancestor worship: it is an offering to the dead so that their spirits will not come back to torment the living. In addition to this, there are sacrifices that create gods, such as those in which a person, or through substitution an animal, is killed to turn a soul into a protective god. When the Yorubas want to make a place taboo, they immolate a human victim or a chicken, whose soul will become the spirit of the place. This is what distinguishes euhemerism from animism, for "if everything in the universe had a soul, why would there be any need to kill a person to give an object a spirit?" Le Roy's monotheism discovers ideas approaching those in Leviticus among the noncivilized: savages consider themselves to be strangers in the world, and they fear using its wealth. Therefore, before taking anything they need, they perform an act of submission to the master of the universe and always offer him the first share. Foucart has defended the theory of alimentary sacrifice according to which sacrifice is always a meal offered to the gods to keep them alive, for if the gods did not eat they would die and consequently the world order would disintegrate. Fellahin probably saw clearly that the statue that was dressed and washed did not really eat, but it was thought that the god was nourished by the spirit of the food.

All these theories tend to unite the many forms of sacrifice in a single principle, which is to be found in the purpose of the ceremony. However, the most diverse purposes have been able to coexist, and the unity sought might be more easily found if, instead of looking at the purpose, we examined the mechanism of the ceremony. This is the approach adopted by Hubert and Mauss.

For them, sacrifice is consecration, the passage from the profane to the sacred. However, it is no ordinary consecration because the person and the god are not in direct contact: they require an intermediary. It can also be seen as an offering, but also not in the ordinary sense. In oblation the object that is offered remains intact, but in sacrifice it is destroyed. This leads to a definition: "Sacrifice is a religious act that, through the consecration of a victim, modifies the state of the person who performs it or of certain objects involved." The example they choose is the Vedic ritual. It can be broken down into the following:

1. The entrance. The initiator of the sacrifice is cleaned of his profane aspects so that he can be born into mystical life. He is shaved and bathed, and, having cast aside his old clothing, he closes himself in a hut where he takes the fetal position. The place and instruments have been consecrated, and the priest, owing to his religious nature, enters into the rite with no prior initiation. The victim is in turn consecrated through aspersions and holy bandages. However, while it does enter into the divine world, it must remain linked to people.

2. The sacrifice. The victim has become sacred, but the power it carries will be able to escape only through death. Thus, after having asked its forgiveness, the animal is killed solemnly, for to do so truly is a sacrilege. The body is then destroyed and brought into relation with, depending on the case, the sacred world (expiatory rituals) or the secular world (alimentary communion). In short, it is linked with the things or beings that are supposed to benefit from the sacrifice, and therefore "the energy that consecration has concentrated on the victim is released through its destruction."

3. The exit. The initiator of the sacrifice returns to the secular world. This explains rituals of deconsecration.

This outline never changes, but its various parts are developed differently, depending on the purpose; for example, in ordination sacrifices the entrance rites are more numerous and in expiation the exit rituals are more extensive.

It is understandable that the profane wishes to enter into communication with the source of life that is the divine. But why must there be an intermediary? This is because the sacred is extremely contagious, and the contagion is dangerous: "If the initiator of the sacrifice were to become fully engaged in the ritual, he would find death, not life. The victim replaces him. It alone penetrates into the dangerous sphere of sacrifice. It succumbs and the initiator remains sheltered. The victim takes his place."

Here there are some fairly complicated ideas at play. Hubert and Mauss consider sacrifice to be a later ritual. They suppose that gifts, simple consecration, and belief in gods came before it and that it is thus incompatible with totemism. Another consequence that can be drawn from this theory is the social nature of the ceremony. This is important for our study. Even if the sacrifice is private, the society is there, present in the form of the priest. Even if the victim is killed in solitude, the society is still present in spirit, since the individual has taken distance from it in order to become linked with the gods.

While this theory does belong to a different level than the preceding ones, it is also vulnerable to objections. It has been criticized as not generalizable because it is based on a complicated ritual that is the work of a learned priesthood with a special idea of the divine (Foucart).

Now we come to the most recent theories. Preuss links sacrifice to the magic of holes. Its purpose would be to make openings in the body so that magical power would flow out with the blood, nourish the elements, such as the rain and wind, and allow them to act. Van der Leuw does not agree with the *do ut des:* "It is inconceivable that people could have made religion a contract before there was trade itself." Sacrifice's mission is to make mystical forces circulate throughout the world not only, as Hubert and Mauss think, to benefit the secular, but to benefit the god, which gathers its creative power from sacrifice. It is only later that the god directs to humans the excess mana it has received from the victim. The sacrifice of the first share, for example, is not a demonstration of gratitude. Instead, it replenishes the strength that the god has lost by making the crops grow and causing the herds to be fertile. For Loisy, sacrifice is not primitive but is produced by combining two prior elements: the offering of food to the spirits and the magical rite of destruction. It begins with imitative actions and initially operates on its own, without divine intervention, though it finally finishes with reverence and worship.

What is our conclusion at the end of this review? It is that the problem of the origin of sacrifice is related to that of the origin of religion. The answer depends on whether one is a euhemerist, an animist, or a believer in another form of religion. Thus we will come back to it. As for the evolution of sacrifice, we see things in the following way. Among the noncivilized, there is a certain ambiguity in religious ideas and rituals. These people are at a crossroads, and we should be wary of overly simplistic schemata. Some of these peoples are caught in magic that is more or less rigid, while others have chosen the path of fertile effort. This can be seen in the notion that the Jews had of sacrifice, which was constantly refined: "Burnt offering and sin offering thou hast not required" (Psalm 40:6); "a broken and contrite heart, O God, thou wilt not despise" (Psalm 51:17).

In India the opposite path was taken. The most ancient Vedas represent sacrifice as a voluntary gift to God. However, we find in them the tiny seed of the idea that sacrifice can work magically, and this is the idea that finally prevails. The Brahmans consider that sacrifice is effective in itself and stronger than the will of the gods.

This is one fact that seems more or less established. There is another one, which can be drawn from Loisy's work: in the beginning there is variety and complication. Durkheim spoke of the functional ambiguity of sacrifice: the schema might always remain the same, but could be used for any purpose. Yet this is not the case. Such ambiguity is not primitive, but recent. In the beginning there was luxuriance, and the role of the priesthood was not to create new forms to be added to the old ones, but to amalgamate the initial wealth into a single whole. This unification was still incomplete in Greece and Rome but more developed in Jewish ceremonies, the Egyptians' divine service, and all Hindu rituals, and complete in the Catholic Mass that maintains the same form, whether the service is daily, with communion, commemorative, Te Deum, and so forth.

All that remains is for us to say a word about the functions of sacrifice. First, it has a religious function: it reinforces the faith and develops religious feeling by bringing people closer to the god. However, its social function is more striking to sociologists. The goods requested from the god through the sacrificial intermediary are above all collective, such as wheat, victory, and fertile animals. The gleaming power of spilled blood rejuvenates family and national ties. Moreover, sacrifice is transmitted by the ancestors and thus enables today's generations to commune with those of long ago by repeating their actions. This cohesive role is especially clear in communion sacrifice and thus appears with totemism: "Among the Waramunga it is even possible to observe totemic rites that are virtually detached from their direct application to the multiplication of totems and make up a sort of liturgical epic in which the traditional life of the clan in particular is asserted in the general economy of the tribe" (Loisy). However, while this feeling of solidarity originates with totemism, it becomes more developed with the cult of the city: Athenian patriotism became self-conscious during the Pan-Athenian festival. The Last Supper established Catholicism and laid the foundations of Christian internationalism.

Rites of Passage and Initiation

A society is made up of individuals who are born, grow up, marry, and die. None of these changes is without effect on the community, which has an interest in ensuring that its numbers do not diminish and that sexual relations are not left undisciplined. Thus all these passages are regulated so that the society is neither harmed nor hindered. In his book on this topic, Van Gennep described these rituals: the physical passage from one place to another, the social passage from one group to another, pregnancy and delivery, birth, initiation of the pubescent child, engagement and marriage, and funerary ceremonies. At first glance, it might seem that the study of these rituals has nothing to do with the sociology of religion, but is concerned instead with social morphology. This is true today, but was not always so. Among the noncivilized, the same person may be sacred or profane depending on the circumstances, for example, when women are pregnant they may be considered taboo and when people are dead they may be seen as impure. It is as if throughout life the individual swings, passing from profane to sacred and back again. The rituals that regulate this movement cannot help but be religious.

Yet we should not believe that all these rites fall into well-defined categories that can be studied separately. They overlap each other to form a whole, and any attempt to divide them is arbitrary. Let us try to show this by taking funerary rites as our point of departure.

Death is not a sudden event, as we conceive of it today. For, as Hertz puts it so aptly, it is not limited to the end of physical existence: it also destroys the social being. The relations that linked the dead person to the family, tribe, and village are broken, but this cannot be done in a single blow. This is why funerary rites have various stages. First, there is a provisional burial of the corpse that lasts until putrefaction is completed. During this time, the bodily soul remains numbly in the body, feeding off offerings while the spiritual soul roams among the living and has not entirely broken away from the earth. Thus the widow may not remarry, and the relatives of the dead are subject to the strictest prohibitions. When the skeleton is completely clean and taken to its final resting place, the soul arrives in the land of the dead. Mourning ends and the relatives return to regular life.

However, the dead do not remain eternally in their celestial or subterranean homes. Most primitives believe in reincarnation and that children who come into the world are returning ancestors. The dead are "brought back to life." This belief is so strong that aboriginals often call children not by their own names, but by the kinship term that linked them with the dead person, such as "father" or "uncle." However, like death, being brought back to life requires several stages. Newborns do not count for savages. If they die, they are not even mourned since they are only "half born" (Lévy-Bruhl). When a baby is given a name, he or she is given a personality because an ancestor is caused to enter into the child. Yet that personality is still vague. The child lives with the women and has a physical, but not a social, existence. He cannot marry or inherit and can be mocked with impunity. Initiation will complete the process by integrating the child into the group of adults.

Initiation rites copy those of death and birth. They turn the young man into a fictional corpse through exhaustion, isolation, and narcotics, and society clearly marks the fact that a new being has appeared by giving him a new name or sometimes by revealing to him his true name, which had been kept a secret until then. The initiate "pretends to be surprised by everything, like a man who has come from another world. He recognizes no one, not even his father and mother." Thus Frazer's explanation:

> Such rites become intelligible if we suppose that their substance consists in extracting the youth's soul in order to transfer it to his totem. For the extraction of his soul would naturally be supposed to kill the youth.... His recovery would then be attributed to... the infusion into him of fresh life drawn from the totem. Thus the essence of these initiatory rites, so far as they consist in a simulation of death and resurrection, would be an exchange of life or souls between the man and his totem. The primitive belief in the possibility of such an exchange of souls comes clearly out in a story of a Basque hunter who affirmed that he had been killed by a bear, but that the bear had, after killing him, breathed its own soul into him, so that the bear's body was now dead, but he himself was a bear, being animated by the bear's soul.... The lad dies as a man and comes to life again as an animal. (Frazer 1957, 905–6)

Frobenius was particularly struck by the role disguises and masks play in such ceremonies. The primary feature of initiation would thus be the transformation or metamorphosis of profane individuals into spirits *(Vergeistigung)*, particularly into spirits of ancestors or of the forest. The purpose of the preliminary taboos and rituals is to ensure that this change or semidivinization will be possible. Thus the young man is inducted into the status of the ancestors and acquires the necessary powers, such as causing rain to fall or healing, in other words, the powers required for society to run smoothly.

The problem with these theories is that they target only one type of society, e.g., totemic groups or those with masks, whereas initiation is a very generalized phenomenon. Moreover, in addition to the rituals of death and assignment of name and masked dances, there is circumcision, subincision, and perforation of the hymen. These are not explained. An attempt has been made to see the latter as hygienic measures (Renan), but this would be to ascribe to primitives concerns that they do not have. Others have seen these practices as substitutes for actual sacrifices of children that are no longer carried out. The Jews, for example, considered circumcision as the sign of an alliance with Yahweh and a surrogate for the killing of the firstborn. However, this is still a recent idea with a priestly origin. Indeed, it seems that these rituals are purification rites and that the blood flowing from the wound releases the bad spirit and allows it to escape. They also appear to be ritual desecrations because the sacredness of the genitals disappears and their use becomes licit. In the virtually Freudian symbolism of the noncivilized, the pulling of teeth is linked to circumcision. They are therefore sexual rites, and here we must disagree with Van Gennep. We must not forget that initiation ends with marriage, which is its legal completion.

While this conception seems to provide a better description of initiation, it is not exhaustive. Initiation is the ritual introduction not only into sexual life, but also into social life as a whole. Consequently, it is accompanied by a form of primitive catechism and an introduction to civic education. In the *engwura* of the Central Australians, which follows immediately after the circumcision or subincision, adult myths and rituals are learned, and the tests preceding it are essentially physical tests intended to strengthen the spirit and produce good warriors (Mauss).

Thus we see that rites of passage overlap. They are complex and include both religious and secular elements. What remains of them in our civilized societies?

If there is one law that is well established by sociology, it is that of social differentiation. Tribal society has disintegrated to give birth to a whole series of independent groupings, such as families, corporations, churches, and the like. What are the consequences of this for the problem at hand?

First, there is a whole series of groupings that have lost their religious nature since mystical life has become the specialization of religious institutions alone. The passage from one secular grouping to another may very well continue with the help of rituals, but they are now profane rituals. Certainly there is a religious marriage and burial alongside the civil marriage and burial, but the religious marriage and burial are no longer rites of passage: they are independent sanctions of civil actions. As a whole, the ideas that supported the ceremonies under study are definitively dead. What remains of them in initiations into corporations (such as the entrance rituals of major universities) and the military (such as reception rituals for conscripts)? Rites of passage no longer belong to the sociology of religion.

Another consequence is obvious: next to these profane groupings there is a differentiated religious society. Entrance into this society cannot be accomplished in just any way. It requires rituals that are all the more regulated because the passage from the profane to the sacred is a change of level. Is this religious initiation the direct descendent of the tribal initiation of which we spoke above? Not exactly, since tribal initiation supposes an undifferentiated society.

However, in addition to and within the tribe, the noncivilized have more restricted societies, such as secret societies. We will come back to this later. What should be pointed out here is that these societies are entered through initiation, which is generally modeled on the initiation into the tribe and involves death, rebirth, masked dances, and revelations. In ancient Egypt, on the east coast of the Mediterranean, and in Greece there were cults of mysteries that can be compared to these societies. There were probably more differences between them than similarities, since one group was totemist and animist while the others worshiped great chthonic or celestial divinities. However, they had features in common, such as a gradual initiation, secret revelation, and an extension beyond national borders. This is the essential point: tribal initiation is mandatory for all members of the tribe from a certain age on, whereas initiation into secret societies is voluntary. When we come to groups with mysteries, we go from constraint to personal initiative. Primitive Christianity is a mystery. Here too we must be careful about excessive identification, for the Christian mystery is a mystery apart. However, since the Church is a differentiated society that is independent with respect to the nation, just as secret societies are outside the tribe and cults of mysteries were independent of the religion of the city, this analogy between situations results in an analogy between the natures of the three cases. The tradition of the Eucharist and the symbol of the apostles remained secret, as did the privilege of baptism.

Thus rites of passage have not disappeared, though they have lost their scope. They have been maintained only in the passage from profane to mystical society and are continuations more of the voluntary, secret initiation into mysteries than of the public, forcible initiation into the tribe. The sequence remains the same: rituals of separation (exorcism and baptism), marginality (the tradition of dogmas), and entry (exsufflation and the laying on of hands). The dramatic framework remains the same: death of the profane man and birth of the new man. Today, however, secrecy is no longer maintained and the ceremony, baptism, or communion is celebrated publicly.

Prayer

Prayer is an oral ritual. Generally, a distinction is made between an individual's prayer, the heart's flight toward a god, and public prayer related to a religion. The former largely escapes sociology, though it is often simply an internalized echo of public prayer, either in its form (e.g., the Lord's Prayer) or in its inspiration, and contains ideas learned in the assembly of the faithful.

Prayer seems to go through three stages in its development. First, it is an incantation: by expressing his desire, the sorcerer acts on the elements or the gods and bends them to his will. The request is effective in itself. By being named, the god becomes dependent, since, as we saw above, its name is an integral part of its personality. Next there is the idea of a contract or bargain, and the prayer becomes a request: "O God, please. . . . O ancestors, we ask of you that . . ." The formula is repeated monotonously, and initially the request is not for spiritual benefits but material goods, peace, rain, or the death of an enemy. To the prayer request are gradually added prayers of worship and offering. This evolution can be followed through the lyric poetry of the Greeks, the hymns of Theognis and Cleanthes, the philosophy of the Stoics, the prayers of Seneca and Epictetus, and also in the Hebrew psalms. However, the "I" of which Israel sings is only very rarely individual. It is most often the personification of the community. Coblentz has noted that of the ninety-two psalms with this form, in forty the "I" represents the Jewish people and in most of the others it represents the religious community. Prayers are "collective, formal, and ritual." Later, the prophets gave them a new meaning that was more spiritual and individualistic. With Christianity, prayer becomes a means of mystical union between the subordinate child and the celestial father.

The rudiments of a few laws can be drawn from this study.

1. The law of hereditary succession (R. Will). Rites that no longer serve a purpose still remain because of momentum. They survive the religious ideas that first accompanied them and endure the most violent ideological revolutions. Therefore:

2. The law of heterogonomy (Wundt). A rite that has lost its initial meaning cannot survive if it does not become related to something. It must be justified by new ideas. In consequence:

3. The law of polytelism (Bouglé). A single rite can maintain a halo of various conceptions around it, and old and new ideas may exist at the same time.

4. The law of liturgical spiritualization (Paulhan). Except in cases of magical change, the various representations always remain possible and range from least to most spiritual. This evolution is related to the progress of moral conscience and individualism. Sacrifice and gifts of food become moral offerings, and prayer and incantation become passionate worship.

We must not believe that this evolution is inevitable or accomplished imperceptibly and gradually. Development is arrested and there are regressions. Above all there are sudden leaps. Thus:

5. The principle of transcendence (de la Boullaye). We will express this principle elsewhere in different terms to avoid preconceptions about the problem of revelation, which must remain outside of science. We will say only that what is superior cannot necessarily be separated from what is inferior, but requires the action of a creative mind.

Progress does not depend on improving actions, which cannot acquire a new nature since the physical always remains physical, but on the religious ideas that explain those actions and become spiritual. However, this does not eliminate the old ideas definitively. They can return if social circumstances analogous to those in which they were created reappear. Here we have a new, properly sociological, law.

6. The principle of the relation of the interpretation of rituals to the social context. This is how Dibelius marked the close kinship between Luther's comments on

the Lord's Prayer and those of the High German catechists in the eighth and ninth centuries. On this point, Mauss writes: "From our point of view, it is interesting to note precisely this return and eclipse of the same interpretation of the same text coinciding with the birth and destruction of purely Roman Catholicism in Germany. The social fact, the ecclesiastical fact, and the dogmatic fact are but one and the same. In order for the Lord's Prayer to again have a given meaning, we must return to social circumstances that are analogous to those it had when it had that meaning."

7. The law of socialization (Paulhan). When the religious beliefs underlying rites disappear, the rites often remain because they have taken on a social character and become collective practices that it would be improper to neglect. Thus, today, baptism and church marriage are for many nothing more than conventional practices, and in the past, atheists celebrated the religion of the city to express their civic spirit.

CHAPTER 6

Organization of Religion

Primitive societies seem to be characterized by the fact that they form relatively small, homogeneous groupings, such as clans. Such societies were initially nomadic; therefore geography was unable to ensure unity. Societies were bound together only by sentiments experienced in common, the sense of solidarity in the struggle for life, which was more or less distinctly the continuation of a social instinct analogous to that of animals. These sentiments are not exclusively mystical. They are a mixture of numerous affective elements that later progress in civilization differentiates. However, almost all have religious tones. A clan is simultaneously and indivisibly a mystical, political, familial, and economic organization. Religious aspects of society cannot be separated from society as a whole. Thus, the same people who calm the sacred terrors, discipline fervor, and direct dances are those who incarnate the political and economic life of the clan: the chiefs. It is as representatives of the society that they celebrate rituals and perform incantations. The religious function has not yet been differentiated. The only beginnings of differentiation in such savage peoples are related to physiology: the separation between the sexes leads to a cultural separation. There are women's beliefs and men's myths, feminine secrets and masculine initiations, and between the sexes taboos raise mystical boundaries.

As people settle and villages appear, we see differentiation unfold, which leads to the formation of independent religious societies. By this we mean secret societies and brotherhoods. This is one of the most obscure points in ethnography because observers have seemed almost to take pleasure in confusing the two. According to Webster, secret societies were at first uniquely political and used as rough instruments of government and justice. Apparently, they became religious only later, when royalty emerged and took over their role in tribal administration. In contrast, brotherhoods would derive from the society of men, from the initial differentiation on a sexual basis already mentioned, and retain both its political and religious attributes. Trilles distinguishes two sorts of secret societies: those of fetishists and those of sorcerers. The former originate in puberty rituals since the fetishists are responsible for celebrating them and therefore rank first in the tribe. However, once the young initiate has entered into the warrior society, he escapes the influence of the fetishist and becomes subject to the chief. In order to maintain their grip on power as it slips away, fetishists organize secret societies. The origin of sorcerer societies is less clear and more properly mystical. Their blood-stained meetings terrify the village and are reminiscent of our medieval Sabbaths.

Thus, among primitive peoples there is not one but a whole series of associations that still perform a wide range of functions simultaneously. However, they are differentiated enough to merit being called the first outlines of a religious society in the true sense. Within the clan they form subgroups that are responsible for celebrating specialized rites for the clan as a whole. The story might be that long ago a spirit initiated the brotherhood's founding ancestor into certain mystical ceremonies of significant social importance since they make rain fall, ensure that the herds are fertile, and so on. Thus, they correspond to the separation of religious functions from other functions in the initial homogeneous group.

As Hubert and Mauss rightly point out, such secret cults could later seem to be in opposition to public religions. In reality, they are products of them, and it is possible to track the evolution that leads to the brotherhood, which is a particularization of a few of the mystical needs of the clan and thus integrated into its life and into the pure religion, separate from the state.

At the origin of the Greek religion there was the formation of brotherhoods, such as the Curetes, Dactyles, Corybants, and Cyclops, that left the men's house charged with specific religious duties to benefit the clans that gave birth to them. The Curetes, for example, were responsible for releasing the fertile power of storms through mimetic rituals (such as imitating thunder by hitting weapons on shields). Likewise, brotherhoods of druids can be understood only if they are compared with those in the Orient (Jubainville) or with the secret societies of the half civilized (Hubert). Such brotherhoods centralized the religious needs of the Celtic people. Many similar examples can be found.

Even with the Christian Church we find this evolution to a certain extent. We will point out the differences later, but this church had to model itself on known frameworks in order to succeed. These frameworks were provided by the Mysteries, which were the only religions with the international character that nascent Christianity wanted to assume. Yet, when we seek their genealogies, the Mysteries, such as those of Bacchus, Demeter, Isis, and Mithra, in turn appear to be ancient national cults that were separated from their nations, religious systems that were detached from their country of origin to become purely spiritual. Here, far in the background, the tribal brotherhood can be seen (Loisy).

Yet we should not dream of a development that is always identical in all places. In China there were also brotherhoods, divisions of ancient tribes, each one of which was responsible for a specific part of the universe and all of which worked together to ensure the harmonious unity of the world. However, they did not give birth to a religion separated from the rest of the social organization but instead served to modify the religious constitution of the country and substitute the cult of ancestors for that of holy places (Granet).

We should also not think that the transformation in the West was long and simple, leading steadily from the lowest forms to the highest. The evolution was creative. Hubert and Mauss may have had an intuition about this when they claimed in *Année sociologique* that while cults of mysteries were related to tribal brotherhoods, we should not talk of an evolution, but rather a whole series of disintegrations and reintegrations: "as they become detached from their social systems, religious ideas and practices *change in nature*" and so give rise to new types.

By specializing in the culture of religious sentiment, brotherhoods tend to free it from the social bonds that imprisoned it and allow it to live its own life. Among the Fan, the sorcerers' societies no longer take into account sexual or social differences. They accept women and include several tribes. Even more clearly, the Greek Erans or Orgeons were open to both men and women, foreigners and citizens, and slaves and free men. In the sacred delirium, distinctions are erased; piety wins out over chauvinism. The links between the participants are mystical, instead of the blood ties uniting the faithful and the protective god in national religions. People are born into national religions, but they enter voluntarily into cults of mysteries. This is the first revolution.

We do not want to discuss the problem of the originality of Christianity. However, even those who consider the new religion to be closest to the Mysteries state "that this mystery is unique and does not fit into the same category. It is not of the same type as the pagan Mysteries" (Loisy). This is sufficient to allow us to use the famous term "creative evolution" with respect to this development. New forms do indeed spring from old ones, but there is infinitely more in the effect than there is in the cause because unpredictable new features appear.

However, religion is never radically separate from society. A religious fringe always remains around social institutions, and the more ancient the society, the greater the fringe. In addition to the ancient Mysteries, there is the religion of the empire, that of the city, and that of the family, and in all of this the religious, the social, and even the political are inextricably intertwined. However, these forms always increasingly tend to disappear, while independent forms gain a greater future. Moreover, as we will show, even civic religions tend toward the independence of the religious function by creating a special priesthood.

Again, referring back to non- or half-civilized peoples, we see various powers concentrated in the hands of the same individuals: for the family, the father; for the tribe, the chief. A differentiated priesthood thus emerges from the primitive confusion. A number of cases must be considered.

According to both Spencer and Frazer, the priest originates in the king. Initially, the king possesses all the powers, both priestly and military. However, as the empire grows, the king is no longer able to perform all his many duties, so he delegates the religious responsibilities to someone close to him. Thus the priest is born. At first, the chief prays to the gods for all families, not just his own, because his ancestors appear stronger than those of his subordinates. Next he may delegate his power, for example to his wife or brother. At first this is done temporarily (Blantyre), and then permanently (as in New Zealand, Mexico, and Peru). In ancient times, the pharaoh was the supreme being who alone could speak to the gods, since he was of their race. However, as the empire developed, he was led to create a priesthood to which he transmitted his mystical powers. In Rome the first kings were political chiefs and priests. The republic abolished only their positions as chiefs, but maintained their status as *rex sacrorum*.

Priests cannot always boast of having had such high origins. They could also be the successors of simple servants responsible for protecting and maintaining religious objects. This explains why, in addition to their liturgical roles, priests have always had deaconal duties (such as cleaning and arranging the sanctuary) and administrative functions (such as managing the god's fortune). Lods sees the Jewish priest, infatuated with himself, as the successor of secondary personages from primitive times. His precursors did not celebrate the sacrifices, which were the responsibility of heads of families and chiefs, but only took care of the sanctuary.

Finally, the last genealogy, which Lévy-Bruhl finds very important, is that involving sorcerers and fetishists with reputations for supernatural powers and for being intermediaries between the human and the divine, especially when their fearsome secrets were transmitted by initiation from father to son, thus suggesting the future priesthood.

Differentiation does not stop here. It continues within the priesthood as it becomes more stable and powerful. In Egypt this led to the separations between the "prophets," justophores, stolists, and sacred scribes; in Babylon between astrologers, magicians, and theologians; and in Mexico between diviners, medicine men, tricksters, and enchanters. Such specialization can only grow over time because new religious needs arise requiring new components. For example, when the Greek religion penetrated into Rome, the college of the *Duumviri sacris faciundis* was created to discipline what could have been a dangerous addition to the city.

Ecclesiastic organization varies widely. This diversity is due to the meeting between two series of causes: those that are internal to churches, operating through spontaneous development or mystical design, and those that are external, relating to the social context in which the religious community develops. These causes interact in such a great variety of ways that we cannot attempt to track the many complex combinations *in concerto*. To do so would be to leave sociology and do history. However, despite their diversity, these combinations have succeeded in establishing ecclesiastical organizations that can be reduced to a certain number of types for which we can sketch a classification.

De la Grasserie makes a distinction between first-impulse religious societies, such as churches, and second-impulse religious societies, such as monasteries and convents. In accordance with their manner of recruitment and also the distribution of power within them, the former include aristocratic societies, in which the priesthood is related to military royalty; democratic societies, in which the priest is elected by the assembly of the faithful; and monarchic societies, such as Catholicism and Tibetan Buddhism, where religious power is centralized in the hands of a single person.

These societies have quite variable degrees of stability, going from the minimum in sects (Russian Orthodoxy and America) to the maximum in extremely hierarchical churches. In sects, mystical life is highly developed but has no set organization. The little group allows itself to be dominated by the secret movements of souls and the unpredictable whims of the Spirit. All sects undoubtedly tend to become more organized as they age, but one of two things happens: either the attempt to organize fails and the sect subdivides and goes down the path of dispersion, or an organization develops and the sect becomes a church, for it is not the number of believers that makes a church but the degree of discipline.

However, organization tends to destroy feeling by crystallizing it. Thus individuals, such as prophets and the inspired, rise up against the priest. Believers quickly rally to them and a new society is formed. Another possibility is that members of a church who wish to experience their faith more intensely may leave the world, retire into solitude, and so become hermits. Since there are generally historical reasons for people to flee the world, the number of hermits increases during troubled or morally corrupt times. Thus, the twin paths of prophecy and holiness produce second-impulse religious societies. These societies also adopt an organization, the importance of which is well known in Catholic monasticism. The rules are similar, but not because they are imitations of each other. They are similar because, despite the differences in structures (for example, between military monasteries such as the Knights of Malta, properly religious monasteries, contemplative and active orders, and mendicant monks), they correspond to the necessities of communal life. Indeed, the degree to which mystical communities are separated from the secular world, or even the rest of the religious world, varies. While it is complete in Catholic monasticism, it is only partial in Muslim brotherhoods, the members of which live with their families.

Thus we always discover the same law at work. This law must be the great law of religious life that leads people, in their communion with mystical forces, to separate and form increasingly narrow groups that become more and more highly charged with religious potential.

At one time, the religious and social links seemed so much the same that the French school of sociology made the former a simple expression of the latter. However, far from becoming one, religious and social emotions that once flowed together imperceptibly have become separate and distinct. Because of its yearning for the absolute, mysticism follows its own path, creating its own structures as it goes, so as to finally result in the individualization of consciousness.

Part III. Religious Systems

The various elements we have just studied never exist in isolation. They form tight syntheses in which they are solidly amalgamated. We call them cults, such as ancestor worship, hero worship, or the Earth Mother cult. Within a nation these cults in turn end up associating among themselves, giving birth to a religion, such as the Persian, Roman, or Australian religions.

But how should these religious systems be studied? Sociology was initially modeled on biology; human societies were likened to living organisms. De la Grasserie adopted this point of view in *Religions comparées*. Like an animal, religion has the faculties of self-preservation and reproduction. It is nourished by daily practices, such as worship, and gives rise to new religions through scission like algae (heresies), grafting like plants (Christianity was grafted onto the Alexandrine doctrine of the Logos), transplantation (Buddhism), and, especially, budding (Protestantism). Religions die of old age (paganism), sickness (heresies), and trauma (persecutions), though it is true that they are sometimes resuscitated (Brahmanism), which is not seen in biology. There are also a pathology and a therapeutics of religions, just as there is medicine of the body: religions suffer from superstitions and scholasticism, which smother them, and they are cured through vaccination (Christianity was inoculated with a little of the idolatry that threatened it) and appropriate hygiene (religion

avoids the contagion of science, which would be dangerous to it).

This simple summary is enough to reveal all that is
arbitrary and all that derives from pure subtlety of thought
in such parallels. It is just as well for sociology to distance
itself from biology and to assert its independence. A new
subject deserves new methods.

Thus the third part of our study will concern religious
societies as special systems that cannot be likened to any
others, since they have their own laws. These systems are
not abstract entities, however. They appear in specific
countries and communities. Perhaps they reflect the color
of the sky or the structure of the group. This will be the
theme of the next two chapters.

CHAPTER 7

Geographical Conditions of Religious Life

Sociology began by looking at geography. When social determinism became an accepted fact, the question arose of what causes could most influence the birth and development of institutions. These causes were thought to be found in the physical setting.

In Montesquieu's work it is possible to see a sociology of religion based on geography. Since hot climates debilitate people, Oriental religions are more unalterable. Since cold climates force people to move to remain warm, northern religions are more likely to change. For the same reason, the number of contemplative orders increases with the heat. Finally, "when a religion established in a given climate clashes too much with the climate of another land, it does not succeed in establishing itself.... It seems, humanly speaking, that climate is what set the boundaries between Christianity and Islam." However, Montesquieu nuanced his thought and limited his explanation. Thus, the penetration of Catholicism in Africa has "despite the prejudicial climate, prevented despotism from establishing itself in Ethiopia."

In France, apart from Renan, who thought monotheism was born in the desert, this point of view has not been very successful, but the English school has insisted on the importance of geography. Frazer writes, "We are more than ever convinced that religion, like all other institutions, has been profoundly influenced by the physical environment." There certainly is some truth in this thesis. The lay of the land influences the location of tombs and temples, such as in Egypt, where the flooding of the Nile forced the Egyptians to place their burial sites far from the river, thus affecting even their conceptions of the afterlife (Moret). Mythology reflects the color of the sky and the look of the surroundings. While Indra's struggles take place in the air, those of Zeus against the Titans trade a celestial nature for a volcanic character, in accordance with the ravaged look of certain Greek mountains (Decharme). "The essential features [of Germanic and Scandinavian mythology] cannot be understood if one's eyes have not been opened to the mountains, forests, fogs, seas, and fields of ice of the Germanic world . . . or if one's ears have not listened to the howling of its storms" (Krappert).

Thus geography is a factor. However, it seems more important when we look to the past. Today we dominate and change nature, whereas we used to be subject to it and were forced to adapt. Totemism is born in isolated places and may be nothing but an effort by primitive people to use taboos as a remedy for a scarcity of food. Yet, closer to us, the Jews have been dispersed throughout the world but still maintain their traditions and rites intact under the greatest variety of skies.

Today, human geography has been profoundly changed, and instead of investigating the action of nature on man it studies the action of man on nature. What does this new human geography contribute to the sociology of religion?

First, we must advise prudence. The present habitat of a people is generally not its primitive one. Migrations and withdrawals have upset everything, and explaining the origin of certain features of religious life by referring to the layout of the local countryside could be a grave mistake. Can the Congolese forest explain the Boschimans when we know they were driven from the African coast? Can the sea explain the Bretons or the Dahomeans when we know they were pushed toward the coast from the middle of the continent? The religion of these peoples surely had to adapt to their new surroundings, but this makes their surroundings a secondary, derived cause, not principal and primitive.

Moreover, human geography is no longer determined by rigid necessities. The land has an effect, but it is not the direct cause of "things." The cause is rather "the human mind in relation to those things" (Simiand); in other words, contingency appears. Thus we come to Febvre's theories of "possibilities and anchor points." The physical environment is not tyrannical: it asks people a question that they answer as they see fit, for example, it has been said that islands are the conservatories of ancient religions. This is often true, especially in the north, but not necessarily so, since Sicily, which is located at a crossroads of maritime traffic, has instead been a laboratory for mystical experiments.

Certain sociologists have tried to prove to certain geographers that the social environment is infinitely more important than the climate. The former certainly admit that geographical conditions exist, but they believe that these conditions never act except by means of and through the social organization. Let us examine the case of the Eskimos.

In the icy land where they live, life is very much subject to the regularity of the seasons. In the summer they live in scattered tents, in the winter in cramped houses where several families crowd in together. In particular, there is the *kashim*, the shared house where men in Alaska spend the cold season, separated from their wives and children. This results in a dual religion: a summer religion, which is private, and a winter religion, which involves communal worship, most of the major initiation and reincarnation celebrations, and strong prohibitions. However, Mauss claims that these cultural differences are caused not so much by differences in climate as by differences in population density. Religious life is less intense in the summer because the group is least dense at that time. Mysticism is unleashed in the winter because all members of the community are reunited and therefore at the mercy of contagious emotions. Thus the season is not the determining factor. It is simply incidental. After long months of communal excitement, Eskimos feel the need to rest and take advantage of the summer warmth to relax in secular life. If the seasons did not alternate, religious and secular life would still alternate, for the mystical rhythm is necessary and would be assisted by other circumstances. Indeed, when the whale hunt forces the aboriginals from the Bering Strait or Point Barrow to come together in the summer, the *kashim* reappears along with all the winter ceremonies. "The seasons are not the direct determining cause of the phenomena they occasion; they act, rather, through the social density that they regulate" (Mauss 1979 [1904–5], 79).

We have focused on this example not only because it was the subject of a major monograph by Mauss, but also because the seasonal rhythm can be found in the lives of many peoples, yet the social fact is always more important than the geographical one. The songs of ancient China prove that the religious life of the Chinese had a seasonal rhythm, but the fact that the fall ritual is the same as that of the spring proves that they are not related to changes in the vegetation. Ceremonies follow the rhythm of peasant life, which has periods when the population comes together and men and women live in different houses, and times when people are scattered over the land. This can be described as the rhythm of work, which requires rest after effort (Granet). The rhythm of rural celebrations in ancient Greece also did not follow that of the life of plants. Those that took place in the winter, for example, were not marked by mourning. According to Granet, they had more to do with society than with climate.

Thus, while the land may act on the religion, it is only one factor among a thousand others, particularly those that are demographic. Thus we will go from the study of geographical conditions to that of social factors. However, before we begin, since human geography concerns more the action of man on nature than it does nature on man, we should say something about religion's influence on the geography of the earth. Febvre maintained that prohibitions prevent people from using things in accordance with their natural needs. However, Deffontaines in particular demonstrated how the mystical mind is made physically manifest in the landscape, thereby changing and humanizing it.

For example, the map of wine production does not correspond to the map of the climate:

> The true original homeland of wine, Egypt, Arabia, and North Africa, no longer produces it because of a religious precept contained in the Muslim Koran. Yet wines were renowned in Egypt and at Carthage. All it took was a change in religion to erase this form of production from the map. Vineyards are now found in temperate countries very far from their place of origin, such as in the Bordeaux, the Loire Valley, Champagne, and the Rhine. There used to be vineyards much further north, in Holland and even in Scandinavia. The reason for this was also religious: Christianity used wine as an offering during mass; it was in a way linked with the vineyard. Wine was spread with Christianity and thus viticultural geography was transformed by the religion. (Deffontaines)

Similarly, silkworm farming could not be established in India because the belief in the transmigration of souls forbade people to kill animals (Sorre). Finally, by studying the facts relating to settlement and population density, we observe "that people's greatest constructive efforts have been carried out in the name of powers that were not terrestrial. It can be said that the preeminent inhabitants of the earth, geographically speaking, are the gods" (Deffontaines).

CHAPTER 8

Social Conditions of Religious Life

Religions appear and evolve within civilizations. They can be neither ahead of nor behind those civilizations without running the risk of perishing. This means that there are links between types of religions and various social structures. Sociology is increasingly interested in discovering these links. Indeed, it even classifies religions on the basis of them; for example, in *Année sociologique* there are clan-based (totemism), tribal, national (Greek polytheism), and universalist (Christianity) systems. German ethnologists have suggested that religions be classified according to whether the people are hunter-gatherers, tillers of the land, herders, or civilized. The former classification is largely related to the group's size, whereas the latter is to its lifestyle. However, the principle is the same.

Yet how should these relations be interpreted? Religion can influence society and shape it according to religious beliefs and thoughts. Likewise, society can influence religion, since it may impose its frameworks, structure, or even form. In both cases the systems will correspond to each other, but the question is in which direction the influence runs and how it can be explained.

In *Cité antique*, Fustel de Coulanges was the first to provide a clear description of the relation between religion and social organization. However, he thought religion dominated organization, with ancestor worship shaping the family and that of heroes shaping the city. In *La Divi-*

sion du travail and *Le Suicide,* Durkheim reversed this point of view: "Religious ideas are products of the social setting, and far from producing that setting. If, once they are formed, they act on the very causes that generated them, their action cannot be very deep." His disciples, in particular Hubert and Mauss, have developed this idea in greater detail. The comparative method reveals how the various religions resemble each other and how they differ. As we have seen, similarities and differences cannot be caused by geography. Neither can they come from the general laws of the mind, mental structure, or human psychological organization, since this does not vary among humans. "Therefore the social setting is the only definite cause of similarities and differences in religious phenomena and their various changes." However, as he himself admitted, in 1895 there was a revolution in Durkheim's thought after a reading of Robertson Smith, which led him to grasp that religious facts were influenced more by psychological factors than by physical ones. This resulted in *The Elementary Forms of the Religious Life.* Durkheim's postulate certainly did not change: religion remained the expression of society. However, it was now the expression of shared emotions that were unleashed during celebrations and ceremonies. It was no longer the expression of social organization. Thus we find that certain disciples of the master returned to Fustel de Coulanges's old thesis. In a conference on the relations between religion and society, Halbwachs showed the influence of religious beliefs on the various types of social organization. Le Coeur concludes his study in *Le Culte de la génération en Guinée* by saying that, "far from the god taking the form of the society, the society is modeled on the religion.... At the origin there is an idea and not simply the physical presence of a large group of people."

These fluctuations in opinion, these contradictions, prove the complexity of the problem. There must be reciprocal action and reaction between religion and social morphology. We will try to separate this dual current of influences in this chapter.

First we will examine society's action.

Each transformation of a society will be accompanied by a corresponding upheaval in its religious systems—for example, the passage from living a nomadic life to a sedentary one. Nomadic Arabs, who are closely knit because of their hard struggle against the desert, worship the ancestors of the clan. Among the fellahin, who are attached to the land, such adoration gives way to the cult of saints, which is more irregular and sporadic. More irregular because celebrations take place only on dates that are relatively widely separated and more sporadic because the tombs of saints are not evenly distributed among the various Muslim countries. The settlement of the Israelites in Judea led to a revolution in the Hebrew concept of God. Yahweh, the god of herders, became a god of agriculture like Baal, while the prophets who withdrew to the desert were more faithful to the former way of living and jealously guarded the ancient religion.

The passage from gathering, which is characteristic of the most backward societies, to agriculture would also be visible in the life of religions. The evidence for this would be found in the passage from rough animism to refined naturalism, either directly, as in America (Müller) or indirectly, as in Africa, through the intermediary of ancestor worship related to nomadic life (Meinhoff).

The transformation of the family system leads to analogous changes. In Greece, the fact that a matriarchy preceded the patriarchy is expressed by legends of women who killed their spouses or their male offspring. The arrival of Apollo and the defeat of the Amazons are related to the beginnings of male power. From then on, women would take refuge in the cults of the Mysteries. The substitution of paternal rights for those of the mother also explains the movement from the cult of the Earth Mother to that of the Sky Father. In the Mysteries, where the Earth Mother was still worshiped, the paternal god forced his way in: Bacchus beside Demeter and Attis beside Isis. Finally, women were even expelled from religions with initiations, to leave only masculine divinities, such as Sol Invictus and Mithra (Dieterich).

The first peoples to become tied to the land were farmers. However, clan rivalry and wars gave rise to cities, which led to a new social structure. This structure was necessarily reflected in religious ideas and organization. The oldest religion that we are able to identify in China seems to be a rural religion, with spring celebrations involving games, jousting, sexual rituals, and love songs. With the establishment of feudal towns, such peasant festivals were no longer sufficient to ensure the natural order. For a city to operate well, all authorities needed to be controlled. Thus the lord inherited the sacred nature of the celebrations, and holy places retained their magical value only by being united with the mystical value of the leader (Granet).

If we go now from the establishment of cities to the revolutions that mark their history, we see that the nobles and the commoners are always the descendants of the conquerors and the conquered, and, since each group maintains its religious traditions, the ethnic struggle also continues in the mystical domain. The final triumph of the lower classes thus leads to a return to ancient ideas that were thought to be dead but had survived in the hearts of the commoners (Pigagnol).

Finally, trade and the development of culture led to a huge intermixing of peoples. Religious syncretism corresponds to this social syncretism, but it is never more than a reflection of it. Therefore, universal religions could have been born only late (Hubert).

Two recent facts, emigration and social density, provide us with another example. The religious differences between the inhabitants of New England and Virginia plantation owners resulted from the fact that the former lived in large cities, where the pressure of public opinion maintained traditions in their greatest purity, whereas the latter were dispersed, which led to a relaxing of social ties and a weakening of religious constraints (some parishioners lived fifty miles from their churches [Boutmy]). The study of the religious behavior of foreigners in Switzerland reveals that emigration weakens religious feeling in most cases, though it sometimes intensifies the interior life of a small elite (Duchart).

While structural modification leads to a parallel upheaval in religious life, the opposite is also true. The permanence of a single social state leads, through changes in dogmas and myths, to the maintenance of a single type of religion. The classic example here is Ireland and Wales. Christianity may have replaced paganism, but the organization of the new church was a simple copy of the organization of the former society. The basic group in these countries was the clan, a small, independent, autonomous community with its own gods and founding heroes, with members who were united by kinship and with a territory that was collectively owned. When it was introduced, Christianity did not immediately take the diocesan, episcopal form it already had on the Continent. First, it established monasteries, each of which was the successor of a clan, so spiritual kinship was simply a continuation of blood kinship. All members of the same community belonged to the same family and the saint played the role of the pagan ancestor. Thus, the ideas were modified but the religious structure did not change.

Yet we can go even further: Were the ideas really changed? The religion of Irish clans was a religion of heroes because Irish society was a society of heroes, and this type of society was no longer defined by kinship or territory alone (though Chavannes claims there were territorial heroes). It was defined by chiefs, kings, founders, and magistrates (Hubert). Since the structure did not change when Christianity arrived, the new religion took on the form of hero worship. This was established by Czarnovsky in his meticulous study of Saint Patrick, in which he shows that the saint was a hero substitute. Thus, different types of societies have different religions and similar societies have similar religions.

Today our societies have become very complex. Within a single nation there are differentiated groups and classes. Religion now varies among groups even though the members of these various classes would recognize themselves as members of the same faith. The Catholicism of peasants does not have much in common with that of intellectuals, but there is instinctive communion, despite doctrinal barriers, between educated Catholics and liberal Protestants. Morphology is stronger than dogmatism (Guignebert).

Thus, religion depends largely on the social setting in which it develops. We must not conclude from this that it is simply an epiphenomenon. Religions survive social revolutions and adapt to completely different social structures while still maintaining their own value systems. One of the conclusions that can be drawn from Frazer's vast inquiry is that totemism is currently practiced by people of very different cultures, such as hunter-gatherer (Australia), farming (Torres Strait, Melanesia, and Polynesia), herding (African Hérero, Bahima, and Banyora), and even industrialized (India) societies. Missionaries have spread Catholicism to the four corners of the earth, yet it has not lost its rigidity.

The reason religion tends to become detached from all social substrates to live an independent life is that it is more than a system of institutions: it is a system of beliefs and sentiments. Since the purpose of institutions is to create harmony in material relations among people, they are strictly subject to demographic and morphological conditions. Insofar as churches are institutions, they are governed by the same constraints. However, they leave more leeway for the aspirations of the heart and intellectual needs. Thus they are less mechanical than other institutions and, as Chevalier says, more effectively register "the secret movements of the soul."

Mystical life can, therefore, reflect social structure for a time, but it ends up freeing itself from, and then breaking, the mold in which it was initially formed. If we return to the example of Ireland and Wales, where the social setting was so clearly imprinted on religious life, we see that the monasteries finally destroyed the clans from which they were born. By preaching brotherhood, Christianity replaced blood ties with mystical relations and by teaching penitence, it put an end to vendettas. By granting monasteries special immunity, it defined spiritual power in opposition to the tribal authority with which it was initially merged. By introducing the use of a last will and testament, it contributed to the movement from communal property to individual ownership (Chevalier). Thus we see religion play a leading role in structural change. The reflection became a cause.

If we want to get a better idea of this action, perhaps we should resort to the famous Bergsonian distinction between closed and open religions. The former, which spring spontaneously out of the human setting to replace failing social instinct, protect societies from possible sources of disorganization. Consequently, their action is primarily conservative. Open religions, which are the fruit of mystical intuition, use their dynamic power to break down borders and shatter conformity. Their action transforms, or even revolutionizes. The former wrap Lazarus in his shroud, while the latter order him to come out of the tomb.

Thus, religion does indeed have a strong influence on the social setting. In order to illustrate it even better, we will survey three different aspects: the physical, demographic, and structural features.

The first example is as follows:

> A dwelling bears the mark of a system of superstitions, beliefs, and specific rituals.... For a long time, the worship of ancestors and household gods determined the layout of homes (generally following a circular pattern). Worship of the gods of the city determined the physical structure of towns (with the citadel or royal palace and temple in the center of the fortifications). The church or monastery, often along with the cemetery, were frequently the focal point of village and urban groupings.... As religious practices lost importance ... the dwelling became less of a focus and the issue of adapting the surroundings to shared aspirations or aversions was considered much less important than ensuring that they were convenient for the needs or desires of the moment, in accordance with the resources available. (Duprat)

The second example is the increase or decrease in the birthrate. This is a demographic fact that also cannot often be explained without reference to a religious factor. In traditional families, religion makes marriage sacred and forces parents to have children. The political instability and misery during the early Middle Ages were caused by major depopulation, but monks worked to regenerate practices and transform forests into arable land, thereby becoming the active artisans of repopulation. If the demographic and religious maps of Europe are compared, "generally, Catholicism coincides with a higher birthrate than that of the countries dominated by Protestantism, which in turn have a higher birthrate than do Catholic countries that have been strongly affected by free thought" (Haury).

In a famous book, Durkheim tried to show that the suicide rate is also a function of religious differences, a thesis that Halbwachs has since challenged. Emigration has causes other than those that are physical (floods) or economic (poor soil):

> Much, indeed most, travel in certain countries, such as in Tibet and Muslim Africa, is for religious reasons. People are drawn to centers such as Jerusalem, Rome, St. James of Compostella, Lourdes, Mecca, Lhassa, and Benares. The geography of pilgrimages is an essential aspect of the geography of travel, and to this we should add religious migrations, repressions of schisms and heresy, religious wars, crusades, and missions. Thus religious facts are responsible for much human wandering. (Deffontaines)

The third example concerns organizational facts, which are more closely related to mystical factors than are movements of populations. Many theories have been advanced to explain the caste system characteristic of India. Neither race nor profession alone can account for it. In order to be understood, castes must be likened to brotherhoods. The separations are prohibitions or taboos and the privileges are magical signs. The proof of this is that while the caste system is really found nowhere but in India, an attenuated version of this system can be seen in other countries, for example in the patrician class of Greece and in the Jewish and, especially, Egyptian priest-hoods. However, the triumph of Hinduism developed what disappeared elsewhere. The feudal system, which is not unique in history and occurs in many places, is also a result of religion. The first lordly authorities seem to have their origin in the winter meetings of brotherhoods, jousts, heraldic fights, and initiation tests in which a mystical hierarchy of powers appears. This explains why the royal emblems in China (such as the dragon and a yellow or red bird) were initially those of blacksmith brotherhoods, masters of fire and lightning. Sorcery transformed the bi-partite division of primitive societies, which are dominated by sexual differentiation, into a feudal organization born in the men's house during seasonal celebrations. Religious transformations have even led to revolutions. The democratization of the Egyptian state was caused by a prior democratization of rituals, "since the secrets of the kings were disclosed, the common folk were admitted into Osirification and, because this ceremony deified them, they were then able to claim their places in the offices and positions of government" (Moret).

Thus two influential currents merge: the social environment influences religion and religion influences the social environment. This occurs within the same population; it is not always easy to separate each current.

CHAPTER 9

Relations among Religious Systems

We have just seen that neither geographical nor social factors can fully account for the constitution of religious systems. Mystical life always tends to overflow, and even change, the context in which it arises. Yet there is more to it, and these factors, though they may be preponderant, are still powerless to explain the differences and similarities among types of religion. This is because, throughout the countries and the centuries, there is necessarily a give-and-take of influences. A series of features is borrowed while others add their subtle colors, resulting in quite profound changes in the initial beliefs and religions.

The most impenetrable groups and most closed communities nonetheless exist next to each other in space. There is always a border zone, where even the most tenacious hatred can never prevent infiltrations and mixtures and where, even in war, there is more assimilation than separation. This means that, to complete our explanation of the organization and development of religious systems, we must now study the various relations among them, as well as the resulting effects.

History and ethnography reveal the extreme importance of these relations. Monuments show how mystical symbols, such as the triskelion and the swastika, have traveled the world over the ages, undoubtedly changing their meanings from one country to another, for a drawing is easier to borrow than a myth, though they both tap a whole series of traditions and beliefs. However, it is certainly more interesting to follow the migrations of a god than those of a symbol. Let us take Mithra as an example, since he has been studied in especially great detail. Mazdaism dates from before the Aryans broke into two branches. Whereas the Indians multiplied the number of their gods, the Iranians grouped them into two rival camps: the gods of light and the gods of darkness. Mithra belonged to the former group, but he was only a second-class spirit. He was only one of the twenty-eight *izeds* and did not figure among the seven *amshaspands* of Ormuz. When the Persians conquered Medea, they fell under the influence of the people they had vanquished. Mithra then gained newfound importance. A new couple was modeled after Babylonian couples: Mithra-Anahita, and the god increasingly came to be seen as a sun god. However, these foreign influences in turn led to violent reactions. At one point, the Persian religion tried to free itself of Chaldean influences. However, it kept Mithra, but freed him of all feminine promiscuity to give him a more austere, ascetic appearance. Then Phrygia borrowed the god from Persia, and he again changed, this time clothing himself as Attis, the ally of Sabazios. Phrygia sacrificed bulls in his honor, as was already done for Cybele. Pirates then carried Mithra to all the shores of the Mediterranean, to Tarsus in particular, where the Roman legions learned about him and soon took him throughout the Roman empire. Later, in his fight against Christianity, Julian gave him some of the characteristics of the opposing god.

In ethnography, the analogical methodology generally employed does not make it easy to identify borrowed features. The antecedent method "evaluates everything a religion possesses at a given time and denounces as borrowed features any later additions that are in any way analogous with surrounding cultures." However, concomitants and consequences must be taken into account if we hope to avoid mistakes. Thus, the historical-cultural method seems the safest. According to Pinard de la Boullaye, it proceeds in the following manner: first, "isocultural" lines are drawn on a map delimiting regions where the same religion is followed, the same material civilization exists, and so forth. Areas with significant overlap between these regions indicate a cultural unit. "Isocultural" lines always reveal zones of mixed influences between such areas. Sometimes, however, there are also analogous cultures separated by considerable distances. How can this be explained? Either by migrations or by the assimilating influence of an environment. If forms that are identical today appear less and less so as we look further into the past, the latter hypothesis should be adopted. If, in the past, even the smallest details were similar, the migration hypothesis should be considered. Finally, there are cases where two religions merge. In order to identify them, Rivers applies the three following principles: (1) If there is no necessary connection between elements, as is the case in Melanesia with the construction of megaliths and sun worship, at least one of the elements arrived through migration. (2) If the elements are closely related, as is the case of megalithic constructions and the sun worship of secret societies in the same area, but the formulas of the ritual are not in the same language, a migration also occurred. (3) If a number of social classes each have their own special ceremonies, each social class represents a civilization with its own religion.

Relations among religious systems can be of two sorts: hostility or mutual penetration. Moreover, it is a curious fact that relations of hostility themselves result in borrowing and infiltration; for example, in order to fight against paganism, Christianity was forced to borrow some of its elements, though it of course modified them. Rivalry thus resulted in imitation.

Hostile relations include, from mildest to strongest, propaganda, such as that of missionaries; persecutions, of which no country has been spared (not even China, the supposed land of tolerance); and religious wars, which can result in the complete destruction of a system or at least its limitation (Protestantism in France).

Religions can also superimpose themselves on one another. Archaeological exploration will then be able to examine one layer at a time until it has dug down to the most ancient foundations. This is the case of the Eleusinian Mysteries, where we find an ancient chthonic religion to which that of the oriental Bacchus and then that of Dionysus Zagreus were successively added.

Gods and rituals can even merge to result in complete assimilation. This is how the Carthaginian Caelestius, imported into Rome in 219 B.C., ended up appearing so much like Juno that Heliogabalus, who no longer recognized the god from Carthage, reintroduced Caelestius in 146, thinking he was importing a religion wholly unknown to the Romans. We are familiar with how the Greek gods were assimilated by the Roman gods (for example, Herakles became Hercules, though they had nothing in common except for a simple phonetic resemblance in their names) and with how the Roman and Gaulish gods were merged.

There are also the many partial mixtures that end up forming entirely new religious systems through the union of heterogeneous elements acting and reacting on each other. The religion of the Cybele-Attis union was dissolved when it penetrated Greece and Cybele was united with Dionysus to form a new divine couple. In India, it is not rare to see Muslims invoke the assistance of a Hindu god and, reciprocally, a Hindu worship a Muslim saint.

The principal agents of these mixtures and infiltrations are migrating populations, which bring their sacred objects and mystical ideas with them. It is even possible to trace invasions of ancient lands by going from sanctuary to sanctuary. Soldiers, such as the Roman legionaries who camped on the banks of the Rhine and the Danube, brought the Matres religion home with them. Merchants carried religious objects among the merchandise in the bags on the backs of their mules or camels. Sailors, of course, and very often slaves also conveyed influences, for example, the barbarian customs of the Moroccan brotherhood of the Aissaouas can be explained by the introduction by slaves of black animism into a mystical Muslim sect. Finally, the role of intellectuals should not be overlooked, as it so often is. Paganism was the foundation of Greco-Roman education and has remained despite the Christianization of the empire, and, since the mind always retains the habits of its first studies, "almost all of antiquity passed through this gateway" (Boissier). In a curious chapter of his book *Das Werden des Gottersglaubens*, Söderblom shows the influence of the Chinese sky god, through the intermediary of French philosophers, on the formation of deism in the eighteenth century.

All this conflict and crossbreeding has had a wide range of effects. Let us mention just a few. When one god is substituted for another, the religious function remains the same; for example, the cult of Christian and Muslim saints replaces and continues that of heroes and spirits. The former god is maintained, though sometimes in a modified form. When Zeus conquered Lycaon, the latter did not die: he was transformed into an epithet (Zeus Lycaios). Another example is the metamorphosis of a religious system into a magical system: medieval magic included all the remnants of ancient pagan religions, and Malaysian magic returns, through Islam, to ancient animism (Skeat). When a religion related to a specific social structure is imported into another social environment, a major change occurs. It becomes a cult of mysteries. This happened in antiquity and in the Orient, where there are phenomena analogous to Indian totemism. This led Hubert and Mauss to suggest the following law: "The mixing of religions occurs mainly through special cults." Asia enters into Latin religions only through the Mysteries, and Christianity was introduced into Indian cults through the intermediary of brotherhoods (Radin). The initial result of all these contacts is almost always a disintegration of the ancient systems. When the blacks from Bahia were transplanted out of their homeland into a different religious environment, their former beliefs crumbled and their rituals were lost. Celtic fairies and heroes are often the remnants of such disintegrations. Yet ancient systems, even when they have been vanquished and encircled on all sides by triumphant churches, can survive, but in secret, in the form of hidden sects. Danon gave an excellent example of this with the Judeo-Christian sect of the Deunmeh (in Turkey). Alternatively, they survive in the form of heresies, as in the case of the Persian *shyysme* and the movements of Africans more or less converted to Christianity or Islam (Harris and Samson Opon in Guinea, the *hamanenjana* in Madagascar, and Mohamed ben Ahmed and Danfidio among the Peuhls). Without giving rise to the formation of special sects, traditions that have been repressed for a time can suddenly spring to life and smother conquering religions. In Sudan, even among the highly Islamized Peuhls, black animism ended up sweeping away Islamic customs and changing them to such an extent that they were almost unrecognizable. What is even more interesting is when two or more systems get along so well together that they give birth to new forms of religion. Wundt shows that when ancestor worship met the religion of animal demons, the result was a religion in which demon-animals take on the appearance of the ancestor and so anthropomorphize (Bantu, Mongolia). This creative phenomenon has even occurred before our very eyes: in our time, Caodaism was born out of the synthesis of three religions in Indochina: Taoism, that is, a religion of the spirits; Confucianism, that is, ancestor worship; and Christianity, mixed with spiritualism.

This chapter has taken us from abstract sociology to the examination of concrete cases, since there is no religion that is not, in the end, the product of these many meetings and conflicts over the centuries. However, other equally interesting relations now require our attention.

CHAPTER 10

Relations between Religious Systems and Other Social Systems

Religion and Politics

The study of the relations between religion and politics was of special interest to the first sociologists, in particular Spencer, who linked it to his great law of human evolution: the passage from the military to the industrial state. He showed the tight relations initially existing between political and ecclesiastic institutions both among ancient and among savage peoples. Priests were simultaneously sacrificers, civil and military leaders, sovereigns, judges, and political advisers. The thirst of their gods was quenched with the blood of enemies. However, with the triumph of industrialism, which accustomed individuals to protecting their own rights without recourse to an external authority and which made resistance against tyranny the supreme moral virtue, in short, which was related to the substitution of cooperation for constraint, the priesthood lost its military and civil functions and kept only its religious role. Spencer's law needs to be better defined, but the schema of differentiation it describes is quite accurate.

First, it is perfectly correct that the two functions, religious and political, are combined initially. It is even possible to see how the latter manages to gradually dissociate itself from the former. There is much evidence for two of the ways that this has occurred.

The Greek king was primarily a religious leader: he performed sacrifices, said prayers, and presided over religious meals. The first Roman kings were also priests. In Egypt, the pharaoh possessed charms, governed the sun, and controlled lightning. The Pharaoh was "he who gives water to the earth," and he used magic to ensure the regularity of the seasons (Moret). The sacred book of the Quichés shows us that in pre-Columbian America, the Indian kings were busy "from morning to night only pleading, from the bottom of their hearts and from deep in their bellies, for light and life for their subjects and power for themselves, as they raised their eyes to the sky." Frazer built his great theory of the magical origins of royalty out of analogous facts borrowed from history, ethnography, and folklore.

In barbarian societies we meet men and magicians to whom the clan attributes considerable influence over the course of nature. Perhaps they cause nurturing rain to fall or help the feeble sun to rise each morning. Kings are the descendants of these magicians; the proof of this is that they often maintain a number of these mysterious powers, such as in Australia, New Guinea, East Africa, and Homeric Greece. However, when religion, which Frazer considers to come after magic, appeared, the priest replaced the sorcerer, and the king, who began as a magician, was increasingly transformed into an incarnate god. The idea of a god present on earth and living among people to help them shocks us today. Yet the numerous references provided by Frazer prove its generality in primitive times. The divine king maintained the functions of the ancient magician. He was still responsible for using mimetic magic to ensure that nature operated properly. His youth and vitality, which are protected against any loss by many taboos (such as the prohibition against touching the ground or seeing the sun), were guarantees of the youth and vitality of the vegetation. Hierogamy, nuptials on the ground itself with the divine spouse, ensured the fertility of animals and harvests. At first, when winter tore the dead leaves off the trees and left nature naked, it was thought that this death was caused by a weakening in the mystical powers of the king. As soon as autumn announced the decline of nature, there was a rush to kill the seasonal king and transfer his magical powers to a vigorous young king of new vegetation before it was too late. However, these kings for a season finally managed to impose themselves and remain, either by ruse or by obtaining a substitute, "who, after a fleeting, more or less effective occupation of the throne, died in their places." These substitutes were successively the oldest son, a minister, a prisoner condemned to death (Mexico), and finally a mannequin (our carnivals). The rupture was then complete: political power became distinct from magical power.

Davy has drawn the attention of researchers to another possible source of the idea of political sovereignty. Primitively, it would be diffused throughout the nomadic clan, where it would be shared equally by all. As people became tied to the land and built villages, it became concentrated in the hands of the chiefs. The transition between these two states would be seen in societies with advanced totemism. In such societies, there is a celebration known as the potlatch, which is the "solemn distribution of food and presents" between the two clans that make up the tribe. Each clan exchanges the things it needs in this manner (exogamy proves that women were originally part of these prestations in kind). Tribal solidarity is created through these regular exchanges. However, the potlatch is not a simple fact of economic distribution. It is also a religious celebration in which the dead commune with the living and totems are distributed and exchanged. Moreover, the potlatch finally splits to give rise to two varieties, one that is still religious (Tlingit) and another that is social, in which individuals use their wealth to impose their authority on others (Haida). When prestations are exchanged, the most generous will dominate, but then the participants engage in a whole series of challenges and competitions (Kwakiutl). Personal prestige thus appears, and, like totems and coats of arms, the dances of the conquered are passed on to the conquerors. The social authority of the future chief does indeed have its roots in the religious privileges of the clan and the totems, symbols, and dances charged with mana that he gradually conquers. "Religion is the primitive category under which everything begins to be described and organized: the establishment of personal power like the rest. . . . In order to establish itself, [political sovereignty] requires certain transformations of religious conceptions of mana and totemism with which, in certain civilizations, the potlatch happens to be related" (Davy).

The myths of the Indo-European immortality festival that we discussed earlier and the ancient Chinese love songs and battles between brotherhoods, to which we alluded, bear witness to the generality of the potlatch and thus the importance of Davy's ideas.

However, even when the two functions are dissociated, they remain linked for a long time, maintaining uninterrupted communication between religious and political systems. First, revolutions occur through religious struggles. The Greek legends of the punishments Dionysus inflicted on royalty emphasize that the rural commoners' struggle against the aristocracy took place within the Dionysian religion. The opposition between the patricians and the plebeians brought not only two classes into conflict, but two religions: the chthonic religion and the religion of the celestial gods. The plebeian triumph coincided with a return to the chthonic religion, which had been repressed for a time. The French Revolution in 1789 began its transformation of society with the Declaration of the Rights of Man that, through the intermediary of the American declaration, was directly related to the Protestant reform in the sixteenth century. Socialist demands rephrase many Christian aspirations in secular terms.

Reciprocally, political authority uses all the restrictive strength of religious feeling in order to become established. When Amenhotep IV, frightened by the ever growing encroachment of the priestly caste, wanted to become the real sovereign of Egypt, he hid his political action behind a religious reform: the replacement of the old national divinity of Amon-Ra by the solar disk Aton. When Heliogabalus tried to create political unity in his empire, he placed it under the sign of the god Sol Invictus and simply repeated a completely spontaneous trend in religious change whereby monotheism goes hand in hand with the centralization of political power. Bantu and Nilotic societies show this in that "the characteristic feature . . . is

a strong military organization. . . . The beginnings of monotheism correspond to this organization" (Mauss's thesis).

Even when there is complete separation between
church and state, political power long retains the remnants
of the time when royalty was related to the priesthood.
Bloch's curious thesis proves this. The king of France used
to cure scrofula. The origin of this power was not extremely old. Christianity had abolished the sacred nature
of the ancient Germanic royalty, but it had not succeeded
in eliminating ancient habits of thought and mystical beliefs. The kings of France intentionally used these beliefs
to their advantage by borrowing thaumaturgical powers
from the legends of saints. The kings of England, Den-
mark, and Hungary also claimed to have similar powers.
The English and French monarchies maintained this tradition for a long time, and Charles X even tried to revive
it again in 1825, right in the midst of the nineteenth century. Moreover, when the German emperors tried to re-
store the Holy Roman Empire, they employed Rosicrucian myths.

Likewise, religious authorities always dream of con-
trolling the political empire. Trilles shows that the purpose of fetishist secret societies is to steal new initiates
away from the authority of political leaders and keep them
under religious control. Among the semicivilized, such
societies play an important role virtually everywhere, even
going so far as to murder and dispossess kings. In a recent
book, Favre points out the role of Freemasonry and Bavarian Illuminism in the preparation of the French Revolution and also shows how Chinese Taoist associations metamorphosed into political associations that played a role in

the revolutionary events in East Asia and through which communism is probably infiltrating China even today.

The Catholic church is primarily a purely spiritual power, but after the fall of the Roman Empire, it appeared as the only real power remaining and took on a political authority it did not originally have. Kings tried to reduce its power, but each time the secular royalty was weakened, the papacy raised its head and tried also to become a terrestrial power (e.g., the struggle between the priesthood and the empire).

We have just seen how difficult it is for the church and the state to become separate. Yet it is a constant rule, and there are two reasons for this. First, because churches become universal and extend beyond the national framework and, second, because within each nation a number of different religions can coexist. Thus, being a citizen is no longer sufficient to belong to a given religion. Membership in the church has become voluntary, the fruit of grace, not of nationality (Halbwachs). Of course, the separation is more or less complete depending on the location. It is very advanced in Christian countries, but only beginning in Muslim nations. There are even cases in which values are reversed, such as in Protestant religions, where the state tends to get the upper hand over the church and imposes its dogma and form on the religion.

We can now classify the main types of relations that can exist between religious and political systems.

Systems in which these two kinds of society are combined are called theocracies. Spencer has provided the main components of the explanation: the clergy's close relations with the divine confer a mysterious authority.

Most often the priesthood is the most cultivated and intelligent class in a country, and power results from the accumulation of property (through donations, salaries, offerings, etc.). This type of organization can have various forms. There is true theocratic government when both powers are in the same hands (Hebrews, Incas, Druids, the Jesuit state in Paraguay, and Calvin's Geneva) or when, though the two powers are separate, the church influences public opinion (as in the Middle Ages). This form of government appears clearly in all monarchies of sacred origin. It appeared in the Far East and Persia and at the end of the Roman Empire because "in such a state, social obedience becomes a form of religious duty" (Joussain).

When the two powers are separate, they still encroach on each other. There are three cases of this: encroachment by the church, which claims a share of the jurisdiction, legal immunity, and the right to crown kings and create political parties; encroachment by the state, which breaks up religious associations and declares perpetual vows illegitimate; and inadvertent encroachment, which is caused by the fact that individuals often belong to two societies at the same time and find it difficult to divide themselves in two. Thus, the Catholic Church adopted Roman law and civil society was later inspired by canon law.

Religion and Economic Life

The historical materialism of Marx and Engels always explains a society's ideological superstructure by its economic infrastructure and takes animal needs to be the driving force behind human evolution. This turns religion into an epiphenomenon without any social importance.

One of Marx's disciples writes that "religion and philosophy would not exist without the economic conditions that make their appearance possible." Christianity owes its existence to the upheaval related to the Roman conquest. Protestantism would not be with us if the bourgeoisie had not appeared. In particular, the land system plays a significant role and accounts for phenomena that are at first sight as mystical as Jewish prophetism and Christian messianism. Thus, dogmas and beliefs simply reflect the vital interests of the social classes, and religious struggles mirror their conflicts of interest.

Next to this materialist interpretation of the relations between religious and economic systems, there is what Weber calls the "psychological" interpretation provided by Nietzsche. Christianity is the religion of the oppressed masses because it responds to and provides a means of expressing the feelings of hatred that slaves have for their masters, while at the same time its dogma of Paradise satisfies the need for liberation and rest, a need that torments the miserable. When Catholicism became aristocratic and allowed itself to become contaminated by the paganism of the Renaissance, Protestantism took up the ancient claims of the working classes. In the end, this interpretation is clearly not far from the first.

We must admit that some of these remarks are sound. Human beings are not purely spiritual. They have bodies and needs and work primarily to satisfy those needs. Thus religion is often only an instinctive strategy to fulfill these requirements. However, it has been said that the influence of such instincts appears, like that of geographical influences, mainly among the most primitive peoples who are closest to our animal nature. This was asserted by Max Weber, one of the sociologists who spent the most time on this problem, when he saw magic as the savage's attempt to bend nature to serve his material interests. Magic is meant to heal illness, produce rain, and cause the sun to ripen fruit. When we are allowed a glimpse of religion, the same interests are always in question, but they are sublimated. According to one of Frazer's theories, totemism could even have a purely dietary origin. The purpose of the Intichiuma ceremony, which is at the heart of Australian totemism, would be to cause the totemic species to multiply, and that of the taboos protecting it would be to prevent its destruction. Of course, this thesis runs up against two objections. First, how could the purpose of totemism be to prevent famine if the clan is not allowed to eat its totem? This may be true, but it can eat those of other clans, just as others can eat its animal, and so totemism could be a form of tribal cooperation through which each naturally helps the other to obtain the food they need. Second, many totems are not edible. However, "while not all totemic species are useful to people, this proves that the religion of these peoples has expanded and passed the strictly utilitarian stage of its beginning. . . . It is strange to note that animal husbandry and agriculture tend to cause totemism to disappear. Do not people then have the power to cause the most useful species to prosper by employing known practical means? Coastal fishers (generally) . . . know nothing of totemism because the products of the sea are inexhaustible"[1] (Descamps). Mythology itself is in some cases a function of lifestyle; for example, the moon dominates the ideas of pastoral peoples and the sun those of farmers because the moon guides herders while the sun causes plants to grow. The Catholic school of sociology that, contrary to what one might expect, gives material interests a primary role and explains most social phenomena by geographical factors and lifestyle, is careful to relate religious systems to economic organization while always attentively distinguishing between those of hunters, herders, and farmers.

Yet the inverse phenomenon is the most common, and has been, even since primitive times. The economic systems of peoples are modified when religions change. We will show this using several examples.

Jevons, Frazer, and Reinach developed an explanatory hypothesis of the origins of domestication that linked it with totemism. When the Dutch discovered Australia, domestication was unknown there. Before the Europeans arrived, the only American animal that was domesticated was the llama. However, the exploration of caves and ancient cities has provided evidence that the dog and the cow have been domesticated for a long time. How is this possible? Obviously, the first prerequisite is that there be wild animals amenable to domestication, such as horses, goats, and sheep. In places, such as America, where there were no such animals, such a technique could not be invented. However, where there were appropriate animals, long experience was required to discriminate them from those that could not be domesticated. Moreover, domestication cannot spring directly from hunting since hungry hunters kill all the animals they find. In order to stop the slaughter, hunters must be restrained by superstitious fears. Thus taboo alone can stay the hunter's arm. Which animals are taboo? Totemic animals. Far from killing them, savage peoples try to keep them nearby, to raise them, for the life and prosperity of the clan are mystically linked to the life of its totem. This would be the origin of domestication. This hypothesis can be defended, but we must recognize with Lang that the facts cannot confirm it; for example, the Bantu had domesticated the cow and the sheep, but they did not count these animals among their totems, which included only wild animals. Meinhoff has defended another theory: the original goal of domestication would have been to ensure a supply of species useful for sacrifices to the gods. At first people would have tried to tame all animals (Asian bas-reliefs show chariots drawn by lions), but experience would eventually lead to discrimination. The Galla raised roosters solely for sacrifice. They never ate them, nor chickens or eggs. The Nyoro milk cows only during religious celebrations once a year. It is an act of communion, and the milk, as a mystical drink, is primarily reserved for priests and divine kings (Hahn). In the end, no matter what the hypothesis, domestication is always given a religious origin.

Allen and Meinhoff think the same applied to agriculture. Primitives turned over the earth only when they buried their dead. Then they threw wild grain, food for the dead person's meals, over the freshly turned earth and poured offerings of water, blood, or milk over the grain. The decomposing flesh and the offerings fertilized the earth and promoted the germination of the grain and luxuriant growth of the plants. It was as if the ancestral spirits were thanking the living for their pious acts. This is why Polynesian yam plantations have the shape of burial mounds. Little by little, wild vegetation takes over and invades the tomb. This is the origin of the idea that, in order to have regular harvests, the same operation must be performed each year: seeds must be sown and buried with a human victim, who will become the spirit of the new harvest and be assimilated into the ancestral spirit that long ago, from the depths of the tomb, thanked the living by ensuring the growth of useful plants. Thus cultivation of the earth would be a direct descendent of ancestor worship. What is true of working the earth could also be claimed with respect to another aspect of agricultural life: grafting. According to Saintyves, the legendary theme of the dry stick that suddenly blooms when a guilty individual has obtained divine pardon would be nothing but the remnant of an ancient divinatory rite that consisted in planting a piece of dead wood in the ground in order to see whether it would sprout in the spring. This would substantiate the innocence or prove the guilt of a person. Thus, grafting would be born of the ordeal and would originally be "God's judgment."

We have already seen how the religious institution of potlatch led to the concentration of wealth in the hands of the chiefs, how the Hindu organization of professional castes was religious in nature, and how Greek corporate associations, such as the dendrophores and the metallurgists, were initially magical brotherhoods. Thus, religion is far from a simple reflection of economic life. It is more accurate to say that the former most often presides over changes in the latter.

Centuries have passed, but the assertion remains correct. Many economists, for example, de Laveleye, have shown that the prosperity of a people is a function of its beliefs: "When we see that Latin Protestants are more successful than German Catholics and when, in a single country and linguistic group with the same origin, members of the Reformed Church make faster, more regular progress than Catholics..., it is very difficult not to attribute the superiority of the former to their religion."

After having established, against historical materialism, that the Reformation was not a by-product of the advent of the bourgeoisie, Weber nonetheless uses statistics to point out that there is a relation between Protestantism and high capitalism. The only remaining solution is that it is instead capitalism that is a consequence of the Reformation. This does not mean that Protestants are more materialistic than Catholics. On the contrary, Puritans have a pessimistic, ascetic view of the world. However, by forcing people to economize, asceticism aids in concentrating capital and, paradoxically, helps capitalism to develop. Moreover, by demonstrating their own salvation through their work, Calvinists fulfill their duties more conscientiously and so become admirable captains of industry.

Weber did not confine himself to studying the relations between Protestantism and capitalism. Other research, particularly on the Hindu and Chinese economies, confirmed his point of view, which was that while capitalism seems at first glance to have purely material roots, it requires a suitable religious environment in order to emerge and expand. This example clearly proves the close union between religious and economic systems, and especially the influence of the former on the latter.

The conclusion that can be drawn from these two lines of inquiry is that, first, there is a primitive *confusion* of the religious, political, and economic. However, this de facto confusion does not entail an identity of nature. These functions are actually very different; indeed, they are even *irreducible*. They are simply mixed together. Social development later untangles the different strands and separates those that correspond to different needs.

Later, from the beginning of their differentiation, there is constant, reciprocal *interaction* among these three systems. The political system uses the religious system, the religious system reflects the economy, and finally the economy and the political system are changed or steered by the religion.

Part IV. The Origin and Evolution of Religions

CHAPTER 11

Theories

When we seek the origins of religions, the first problem is that of how far back we should go. In *The Origin of Civilization and the Primitive Condition of Man*, Lubbock asserts the existence of an initial stage among the most backward peoples where there would be absolutely no religion. However, later explorers have proved all his examples to be unsubstantiated, and nothing at all remains of the supposed atheism of primitive humanity. In contrast, Comte, Guyau, and especially Van Ende have tried to identify the seeds of mystical feeling even among animals. The seeds would be found, for example, in the terror beasts feel when faced with cosmic catastrophes or the approach of death and in the mute adoration of human genius. These theorists have even sketched out a kind of fetishism. However, contemporary psychology generally rejects these superficial analogies. Religion is a purely human fact. It alone is characteristic of all humanity. Thus, would not the role of the sociology of religion be to trace the mystical scope of social evolution? This has long seemed to be the case, so we must say a few words about the various theories that have claimed to define this scope.

For Comte, the founder of sociology, the scope of religion follows part of the same path as the evolution of the human mind. Religion, a product of the intellectual need innate to the human species, appeared immediately. First it took the form of fetishism (this word is borrowed from Charles de Brosses), which instantly makes every object (a tree, a rock, a spring) divine by ascribing mystical power to it. Prepared by astrolatry, which is an intermediary state, a revolution took humanity from fetishism to polytheism. Comte says that this was a revolution and not a simple evolution because in the former state matter is active while in the latter it is inert and the gods are exterior and superior to it. Progress in observation and the desire for a single explanation of the world led to monotheism. This was structured in the Catholic framework, which was later destroyed by Protestant criticism, thus preparing the way for the final positive state. Thus the great law of religious evolution, later inherited by Durkheim, was already the law of the continual decline of theological thinking.

However, was there no room for an intermediary position between the Christian theory of objective revelation, which did not appear sufficiently scientific to researchers, and Comte's gross fetishism? Max Müller, for one, thought so, and, beginning with knowledge, rich for the time, of recently discovered Sanskrit literature, he placed a kind of subjective revelation, an intuition of the infinite, at the origin of religion. Religion would be nothing but the language people use to translate this confused impression of their senses and their hearts. Thus, it would first take the form of henotheism or kathenotheism. These words indicate that a multiplicity of gods (Indra, Varuni, Agni) is recognized, but that each time one of them is worshiped, that god is immediately perceived as the most powerful of all, receives the attributes of the others, and is considered unique. The reason for this is that worship hints, more or less confusedly, at the infinite that is beyond the gods and yet symbolized by them. Müller lived long enough to see evolutionism penetrate ethnology and destroy his theory; the idea of the infinite is the work of the Hindu priesthood and relatively recent. Kathenotheism appears only in exceptional circumstances and in countries that are already civilized.

The concept that derived from Müller's work has been called "naturism" and can also be found later in the astral school of German mythologists. Naturism sees religion as the human mind's first attempt to explain natural phenomena, particularly those that are surprising or frightening, in other words, Müller's movements of the sun and the Germans' various phases of the moon. Durkheim's refutation of naturism has become classic: "that which characterizes the life of nature is a regularity which approaches monotony... and uniformity could never produce strong emotions" (Durkheim 1915, 84 [1912, 119]). Primitive people do not feel oppressed by cosmic forces. On the contrary, "a primitive attributes to himself an empire over things [here Durkheim is alluding to magic] which he really does not have" (Durkheim 1915, 86 [1912, 122]). Finally, the stars were made divine only very late. "The first beings to which the cult is addressed... are humble vegetables and animals, in relation to which men could easily claim an equality: they are ducks, rabbits, kangaroos, lizards, worms, frogs, etc." (Durkheim 1915, 86 [1912, 122]). This last argument can be challenged, as we will see later. However, when Durkheim used it, it seemed decisive.

Moreover, aside from the German astral school, those who endorsed naturism were relatively few compared with the partisans of animism, a doctrine that we will discuss at greater length. This theory has two branches: Tylor's animism, properly speaking, and Spencer's manism. While *Principles of Sociology* came out a few years after *Primitive Culture*, we will nonetheless start with manism since it is a specific case of animism.

The first conception of supernatural beings that can be discovered, says Spencer, is that of the spirits of the dead, an idea born of dreams that present us with images of ghosts or originating in the desire to make sense of cataleptic states, explicable only in terms of the soul leaving the body momentarily. Primitives perform propitiatory rites for these spirits, and this is the origin of ancestor worship, the first of all religions. Fetishism derives from it (fetishes are initially pieces of mummified corpses kept as relics), zoolatry (animals seen near the hut where the corpse lies are considered to be metamorphoses of the soul of the dead person), plant worship (either the madness caused by ingesting certain plants is explained by spirits that are supposed to be contained in them, or plants growing on the tombs of ancestors are supposed to be incarnated spirits), and finally nature worship (initially nature is revered as the resting place of the dead and then in itself, by affective transfer). Thus naturism, far from being primitive, as Müller thought, would instead be a later, derived phenomenon. The first gods have always been ancestors, which is the reason for the name given to this doctrine, euhemerism, in memory of the Greek philosopher, Euhemerus, who explained gods as the deification of dead kings.

The most powerful criticism of this theory is that it has confused funerary rituals with ancestor worship. The latter is generally recent and often even presupposes a strong patriarchal organization. The former are more general, but they do not necessarily lead to manism. Thus we come to Tylor's generalized animism. However, before discussing it, it should be noted that manism was taken up again in 1897 by Grant Allen. In contrast with Tylor, he did not believe that in primitive religions all objects in the universe were thought to have a soul. On the contrary, when a primitive wants to make an object or place taboo, he sacrifices a person or an animal there in order to use their disincarnate spirits to protect the place or object. This means that gods are always at the origin of manes. Marillier has demonstrated that in order for manism to exist, naturalist mythology must be expelled from religion, which is proof of the error because there is no religion without myths. The gods of natural phenomena are not the souls of the dead. They belong to classes and races other than those of men. Even when anthropomorphism later lends them a human appearance, they are considered to be glorified men who are alive, not shadows.

Tylor tried to reconstitute the primitive mentality. He showed how thinking about sleep and experiencing trances led men to the idea of a soul that left the body. In accordance with the ideas conveyed by their dreams or visions, this soul was conceived of as more ethereal than the body. Primitives dwelled in the midst of living nature: running water, blowing wind, and so on. Thus they considered everything, animals, plants, and objects, in terms of their own activity. Everything had a body and a soul. In their eyes, the world was peopled by an infinity of spirits, such as spirits of springs, trees, and mountains, which is the origin of the name given to the theory: animism. The gods of polytheism would be simply a selection and promotion of a few of these spirits, all of which used to be feared and worshiped indiscriminately.

Animism was very successful and quickly became the top theory in the sociology of religion. However, criticisms gradually emerged. The argument from dreams, which was at the foundation of Tylor's construction, was no longer accepted because the images that dreams present are incoherent; for example, the dead can appear in them in the form they had when they were children and not necessarily in the form of cadavers and, above all, because the noncivilized do not believe in the reality of all their visions. They distinguish those that are meaningful and revealing from those they hold to be illusory tricks of their imagination. Moreover, the soul is considered by the savage to be invisible and fluid, whereas images in dreams present the dead as physical and tangible.

Above all, ethnography has revealed the complexity of notions that primitives have of the soul. We have shown in a preceding chapter that for primitives there is not one but several souls. More precisely, according to Lévy-Bruhl, an individual participates in a series: the name, the shadow, and the totem. These coexist simultaneously and crisscross each other without melting into the clear consciousness of truly single individuality. Animism supposes an individualist conception of the self, but it seems that this notion of a psychic self, which Tylor takes as the foundation of humanity's intellectual evolution, is in fact something of which the savage is completely ignorant. He cannot project a soul into nature because he has never felt his own soul.

However, the most closely argued criticism of animism is Durkheim's. He says, "What does the dream amount to in our lives? How little place it holds, especially because of the very vague impressions it leaves." Why would it not be the same for the savage? "Of the two existences which he successively leads, that of the day and that of the night, it is the first that should interest him the most" (Durkheim 1915, 58 [1912, 82]). Moreover, a soul seen in a dream is not yet a spirit. It becomes so only once death has freed it from its earthly body to give it an independent existence. But why would death have this power to deify? "Death adds nothing essential to it, except a greater liberty of movement" (Durkheim 1915, 61 [1912, 85]). Furthermore, not all souls of the dead are worshiped indiscriminately. In other words, the simple fact of dying does not necessarily lead to divinity. From the idea of the soul, Tylor goes on to that of the spirit of nature. Durkheim's criticism follows him into this field: "If the spirits and gods of nature were really formed in the image of the human soul, they should bear traces of their origin and bring to mind the essential traits of their model" (Durkheim 1915, 67 [1912, 94]). Yet the soul is considered to reside within the body, whereas spirits visit waters and woods but are external to them. A soul seen in a dream has a human shape, but anthropomorphism occurs late, and the first gods resemble animals. Finally, if animism were built on illusions from dreams, religion would be a vast aberration. How, then, could it have been perpetuated as intelligence progressed? The fact that it has remained must mean it corresponds to some hidden reality.

Durkheim's criticism did not kill animism. It simply forced it to undergo revision, and it now survives in new forms in contemporary thought. Nieuwenhuis, who conducted a study in the Malaysian archipelago, identifies in Durkheim's arguments a series of questions that animism must answer if it hopes to be justified in the eyes of science: (1) Since animism is based on the notion of soul, how could that notion have been formed? (2) How was it then applied to objects in nature? (3) Why were these spirits worshiped? (4) Given that there is no religion in which ancestor worship stands alone, how did the religion of nature derive from it? Nieuwenhuis begins with Hamilton's principle: nothing is born of nothing and nothing can come from nothing, a principle that would be innate to all human minds. Since the primitive cannot conceive of the idea of nothingness, all objects must be permanent. When a person dies, life does not therefore disappear, in other words become nothing. It must continue to exist, which is the origin of the idea of the soul. This concept probably undergoes later developments and becomes more complicated, thereby providing the same individual with many souls. Study of the Malaysians, in any case, has shown that all such complications have their origin in this very simple point of departure. But then how were souls given to objects in nature? The transfer that seemed so incomprehensible to Durkheim is not really so if we always use the same principle. In the world there are a multitude of forces and energies. These forces can neither come from nothing nor fall into nothingness. They require a medium, a spirit. Thus Durkheim's criticism of Tylor is correct: the point of departure cannot be the fictions of a dream. However, animism regains all its value if we make it rest on a rationalist conception of the world, for it then ceases to be an aberration. However, these forces of nature release terror (thunder, lightning) or joy (needed rain) in the soul of the primitive. This leads to the idea of appeasing the spirits that control the forces of nature, and this in turn gives rise to a dual religion: the worship of natural phenomena and of ancestors.

Despite these corrections, the discovery of the notion of mana, which we analyzed earlier, was to stimulate new research and give rise to another system, preanimism, which was first held by King, Marett, and Preuss. According to it, animism would be preceded by a state in which the savage would not yet have formed the idea of a personal soul, but would believe in a diffuse force throughout the universe, and thus magic would come before religion. However, Preuss breaks the notion of magical effectiveness into a series of singular properties: the magic of openings (defecation, sex, breathing, speaking), the magic of cries and songs, and the magic of dances; whereas the two English ethnographers consider humanity's initial religious idea to be that of an impersonal power spread out in things. Individual spirits would be born of a particularization of mana as it condenses and becomes concrete in certain objects or beings.

We will not spend much time on this thesis because, as we have seen, it is based on a mistaken conception of mana. We refer the reader to Lehmann's analysis, which we summarized earlier. However, even if this conception of mana were correct, it would still seem strange that humanity would have begun with the idea of an impersonal force. This idea appears very difficult for the brain of a primitive to form because it is too theoretical.

Durkheim's sociological theory deals with this difficulty. He begins with preanimism, but tries to prove that the idea of mana came first by explaining its origin. We must focus on this point because a book on the sociology of religion naturally must give precedence to theories overtly claiming to be sociological. Durkheim's discussion starts with Australian totemism, which he defines as the clan members' worship of the plant or animal they consider to be their ancestor. However, when examined more closely, totemism is not really the worship of such plants or animals. They are only symbols and clan insignia. The religion passes through them to the anonymous force of which they are the vessel. Thus, if the totem is both the mystical power and the emblem of the society, perhaps the god and the society are one, and the totem "can therefore be nothing else than the clan itself, personified and represented to the imagination under the visible form of the animal or vegetable which serves as totem" (Durkheim 1915, 206 [1912, 295]). This assimilation of the god with the group is justified by the argument that the society alone "has all it needs to awaken the feeling of the divine in people's minds." Like a god, it constrains and obliges and is also "a force upon which our strength lies" (Durkheim 1915, 209 [1912, 299]), a reservoir of inexhaustible energy. This makes it understandable that religion has persisted throughout civilizations. It corresponds to something real, to the social existence, which is a universal, permanent fact. However, one question remains unanswered: How could the feeling of community have metamorphosed into an impression of the divine? The answer to this lies in the fact that the clan assembles for intense rituals during totemic ceremonies. The communion of people participating in the same rites generates extremely strong collective emotions, and when the individual returns to a calmer state he has the impression that he has fallen from a world where he lived more keenly. That world of fiery emotions will be what he will call the sacred world, and mana will be only the hypostatization of the emotional power.

Let us add, however, that for Durkheim the idea of mana is only logically, not chronologically, prior to that of individual spirits, for just as there are no societies without individuals, there can be no mana without individual souls.

In summary, for Durkheim and his school, neither dreams nor contemplation of nature can engender the feeling of the divine because they are facts of common experience, but the sacred is beyond experience. Thus its origin must be external to humans, in other words, social. However, what Durkheim says against dreams and nature can, as Delacroix justly notes, be turned against him, for society is also a natural fact. Thus, real society, with its frameworks and organization, cannot be an object of faith. What is required is an ideal society, forged within the soul steeped in values. Yet here the individual reappears. If we consider that it is not society itself but great communal excitement that is the real source of the divine for Durkheim, the difficulty does not disappear. It only changes, for why would not the same apply to individual mysticism and the solitary trembling that throws the inspired into a trance? As Dussaud says, "If a trance is a necessary condition for man to feel something in nature that is powerful and external to him . . . it should be noted that this exaltation can be reached just as well through solitary meditation as in society." This applies to noncivilized peoples, as shown by recent work by Steinmetz and Malinowski on primitives in general and by Beck on Australians in particular, among whom the individual plays quite an important role. The priest often owes his relatively privileged position to a veritable personal vocation; initiation rites, which are often celebrated in retreat and solitude, may be governed by society, but they often cause individual mysticism; and, finally, religion generates truly personal experiences for some people. Psychology, at least as much as sociology, holds the key to the divine secret.

The various theses that we have just reviewed all share one thing: they are all evolutionary, and thus in contradiction with the dogma of primitive revelation. Yet not quite, for it is possible to hold that, because of original sin, the effects of divine revelation were quickly forgotten and humanity had to begin again at zero in its journey toward monotheism. This is why Catholics such as Bros have been able to subscribe to animism. However, in 1898 Lang published *The Making of Religion*, which exploded like a bomb in ethnography. In it he argues (1) that all people have the idea of causality and that this idea is sufficient to lead to belief in gods that are "makers" or creators of the world; (2) that among all peoples, ancient and savage, we find faith in an immortal Father, God and Author of all things, side by side with obscene and grotesque myths; and (3) that, primitively, the religious factor arises in a state of great purity and the mythological element later smothers that initial feeling. Tylor's animism would provide the explanation for the mythological element.

Lang's ideas remained something of an exception until the historical method arose in ethnography. It seemed this method would be able to confirm the theory. The historical approach begins with the methods we have already indicated to try to determine cultural zones on the world map. Once they are clearly delimited, they are classified chronologically using various criteria, such as those of necessary presupposition (reactionary institutions suppose the preexistence of a state of things against which they react), penetration (the incorporation of a rite from a civilization requires time, so the more fully incorporated a rite is, the older it is), social associations (since initiatives originate in the cultivated classes, the beliefs of the lower classes are generally older), and so forth. These criteria would make it possible to identify a chronology of cultures among the noncivilized despite a lack of dates.

However, according to the most qualified advocate of primitive monotheism, Schmidt, the further back we go in primitive civilizations, the more clearly we see the idea of a great god, the supreme creator and judge of morality:

> If we encompass in a glance the distribution of primitive civilizations and their shared belief in a supreme being, we realize that it is not at all something insignificant or uncertain. Initially, these civilizations encircled the

southern half of the ancient world like a belt, a belt that the Ges-Tapuya extended to the New World. Their present isolated relegation to islands, the extreme edges of continents, the hearts of mountainous regions, and the interior of virgin forests attests to an earlier distribution that was much more dense and continuous. In second and third place, they spread to the extremities of the earth, along with the Arctic and meridional cultures. It is clear that none of the more recent civilizations has managed such a geographical expansion. If, now, we accept that faith in a Supreme Being appears everywhere, we will likely admit that this faith is an essential part of the most ancient human civilization.

Schmidt's documentation may not have all the weight he accords it. Lowie, who independently investigated primitive belief in a great god in *Primitive Religion*, concludes that the pieces of evidence available to support this belief are "so vague, fragmentary and contradictory that nothing positive can be drawn from them."

However, let us accept that there is definite proof supporting this belief. Would Schmidt's conclusion then be substantiated and could we really speak of primitive monotheism? Most sociologists would reject this. Goblet d'Alviella notes, "It must be observed that in all identified cases there is a supreme god but not a unique god, which is completely different . . . ; the notions of infinity, absoluteness and perfection, which are the necessary attributes of a unique god, are beyond the understanding of savages." Many of these great gods are *dii otiosi*, in other words, distant gods who are not interested in humans and are therefore not worshiped (Söderblom). As for those that are the objects of prayers or sacrifices, the word they suggest is *monolatry*, not *monotheism*. Thus we come to a final theory, which I will call synthetic or eclectic, that was developed by Söderblom in *Das Werden des Gottersglaubens*.

According to this theory, the idea of God has three origins, and its evolution is also threefold. Among primitives we find simultaneously animism, or rather animatism, which simply considers objects as living or not, whereas animism mistakenly considers them to have spiritual power; an impersonal power or mana, related to taboo; and finally creative gods. The idea of spirits is not strictly religious but rather the savage's first philosophy. The impersonal power produces rituals and is thus more truly mystical, yet it is never worshiped in itself as a divinity. Finally, the great gods are not the subjects of organized religion. Three lines of religious evolution spring from this "vestibule": the great gods come from the celestial divinities (the great Chinese god), from mana (the Brahman pantheism in India), and from animism (Jewish monotheism).

Which of these very different theses should we choose? No dialectical argument is sufficient, and in any case, logic must defer to the facts. Thus we have to consult historical and ethnographical data.

CHAPTER 12

Historical and Ethnographic Data

The method usually followed when studying social dynamics consists in beginning with a society that is supposed to be simple, crude, and primitive and then tracing the steps to present civilization. We consider this approach to be dangerous because the initial society is generally more hypothetical than real. Instead, we will take the opposite approach and go backward through the centuries. As we go from best known to least known, we will use historical data and stop where documents and vestiges end in order to leave as little room as possible for fantasy and arbitrariness, which have been the downfall of so many sociological constructions.

In the great Western nations, religion is monotheistic. It is the most thoroughly studied type of religion because it is still living in beliefs and institutions. Yet, what uninformed eyes first see is the extreme difficulty monotheism has in maintaining its purity, as if there were an ineluctable inclination leading people to increase the number of divine individuals. Angels, devils, saints, "the gods' successors," as they are called by Saintyves, maintain a kind of latent polytheism among the working classes. Thus, perpetual vigilance is required in religion to maintain monotheism. Its advent was prepared by the last centuries of the Roman Empire. At that time a syncretism was produced in which all the gods tended to merge into one. Not, of course, the gods of the cities, which remained local, but the great gods of nature, such as Zeus, and the savior gods, such as Bacchus. Boulanger has shown that the law of this syncretization has three stages: the association of several gods in prayer, where their individuality is effaced; then assimilation; and finally, under the influence of the Orient, the appearance of pantheistic gods, with the various deities no longer considered to be anything but different aspects by which the supreme, infinite Being is revealed. However, the triumph of Christianity stopped the march of paganism toward divine unity, and our monotheism comes directly from that of the Jews. Yet here again, in the first books of the Bible, Yahweh stands out while the Elohim remain in the background. Thus, historically, modern monotheism was indeed preceded by polytheism everywhere.

However, dualism is sometimes set between polytheism and monotheism. Foucart has studied this and shown that such dualism is not a primitive phenomenon, but almost always the work of an organized priesthood. This is very clear in the case of Mazdaism. Originally, the god had a physical appearance and symbolized the struggle between material elements, such as the Earth and Heaven. Then social features were acquired and the struggle became one between the national gods of two peoples: the conquerors and the conquered. Finally it took on a moral appearance, in the form of the struggle between good and evil. Like polytheism, dualism thus tends toward monotheism, with the good gods infinitely more powerful than the diabolical, which are reduced to an increasingly inferior position.

Polytheism is well known in comparative mythology. As we mentioned with respect to dogmas, religious ideas are subject to two kinds of laws: mystical and sociological. This is also true of myths, as is revealed by the study of polytheism. An example can be seen in the mystical laws: that which governed the gods of the mysteries divided one god into two and then into three. Thus, Bacchus divides into a bearded god and an effeminate god, and then he is born three times, the third time under the wine press. At Eleusis, a mother goddess was worshiped who later divided to produce the Demeter-Persephone duo, to which a third subordinate divinity was later added. The mystical work is further complicated by the union of male and female triads that give birth to other compound groups: father, mother, and child. Then religious feeling turns the child into a sacrificed god, or a teacher of man, or an intercessor. While we have taken Greece as an example, the phenomenon is universal. Triads are found in Egypt, with Isis, Osiris, and Horus; in India, with Brahma, Vishnu, and Shiva; and in pre-Columbian America.

Sociological laws result in the formation of divine pantheons. In Egypt, each clan had its patron god. Domination by the victorious clans and federalism led these multiple gods to be associated with each other and to form families, and thus Egyptian mythology was first a reflection of political rivalries and alliances (Moret, Foucart). The same thing happened in Greece. The reason that the legends ascribe so many adventures to the gods is simply that Zeus, Apollo, and Herakles were the result of the association under a single name of several local gods called Zeus, Apollo, and Herakles. Polytheism is thus already the effect of an initial social syncretism. However, this synthesis is not alone and, as Farnell rightly saw, analysis also creates new gods by fragmenting old ones. Pandora, Aglauros, Demeter, and Core would all come from Ge.

Until now, we have confined ourselves to urban civilization. History does allow us to go back further, but with greater difficulty because documents are rare and can be understood only through interpretation. Thus, archaeology and linguistics now come into play. Employing a linguistic approach, Usener discovered that personal gods were preceded by special gods *(Sondergötter)*, not personified abstract qualities, but gods of each stage of life: the Roman *indigetamenta* (gods of birth, the first cry, the first step, etc.), the Lithuanian gods, and even the first Greek divinities, which have an adjectival form. Further back, he glimpsed momentary gods *(Augenblickgötter):* the god of the last sheaf of wheat, the god of the lightning flash, the god of each day's moon. Thus, originally there were thousands and thousands of gods, since each phenomenon had its own. Names created gods. They made what was initially only the experience of a transient sacred power into something concrete and material and thereby gave the experience the permanence required for use by mythopoetic fantasy. Archaeology shows that the Greek civilization was preceded by the Aegean civilization, and Aegean monuments enable us to follow the transition from fetishism to polytheism. The stone post, the double-headed hatchet, and the like were first worshiped in themselves, but then became the perches of the sacred bird or the attributes of the mother goddess—in short, simple symbols (Glotz). Dieterich has described the primitive meaning of the mother goddess, whose importance and steatopygic shape are seen in Crete. The earth was above all the sojourn of the dead seeking reincarnation. It long remained a custom to place a newborn on the ground so that the soul of a dead person could enter the child's body. Thus, the Earth truly was the Mother. However, this discovery takes us from nature to the spirits of the dead, from naturism to animism.

Fustel de Coulanges saw the most ancient foundation of pagan religion in ancestor worship. The Aegean civilization was not ignorant of this religion, as the form and orientation of its tombs and the objects buried with the corpses show. Thus, historical data authorize us to postulate a simultaneous awakening of the cult of nature and of worship of the dead, and, if we absolutely require a chronology, we can suggest that the latter preceded the former.

While historians continued their research, ethnographers and folklorists discovered new types of religions, such as agrarian religions, brotherhoods, and totemism. Naturally, historians and sociologists wonder if it might not be possible also to find such religions in the history of antiquity. Let us have a look at the conclusions of their research.

Frazer begins with the sacred nature of primitive, Greek, Roman, and oriental royalty. Where did it come from? From the fact that these kings were the descendants of man-gods, whom we have already mentioned, incarnations of agrarian demons and representatives of the new and then the old vegetation, who were ritually killed. Traces of this remain in the myths of Osiris, Demeter, and Romulus. Prior to this there is evidence of animals being killed in the fields after having been rolled in the last sheaf, such as the wolf of the wheat and the goat of the grain. Their remains fertilized the earth and brought prosperity. Thus, the realm of magic supposes agrarian cults, which lead us to the threshold of animal religions, which might be cases of totemism.

Gernet wants to see three successive layers in Greek religion: a polytheist religion of the cities; an earlier religion of magical brotherhoods, such as the Curetes and the Dactyles, which were analogous to the secret societies of primitive peoples and products of a division of a prior tribal religion; and, earliest, an agricultural clan religion with seasonal celebrations. Granet glimpsed the same stratification in China. This hypothesis is sufficiently substantiated; thus we have used it above.

The totemist hypothesis is, in contrast, very controversial. Wherever the Greeks and Celts associated an animal with a god, Reinach tried to see the traces of primitive totemism. However, Mauss notes that this reveals some confusion between totemism and zoolatry because, as we will soon see, totemism recognizes an animal as the ancestor and protector of the clan, but never as a god. The emblems of neolithic Egyptian villages, seen on vases in the form of the images of falcons, vultures, greyhounds, and scorpions, which later became attributes of the pharaonic royalty, are viewed by Loret and Moret as ancient totems that were transformed into gods through confusion with the ancestral patriarchy of the clan. While this thesis is on more solid ground, it remains hypothetical because no trace has been found of the foundation of totemism: belief in the kinship of a group of humans and a species of animal. Renel thinks that among the Romans, the religion of emblems with animal figures is a remnant of ancient Latin totemism. Perhaps there is indeed an element of totemism in this, but totemism is an extremely complex organization, and it is at least premature to derive from the existence of one of its elements the existence of all the others.

The work of Glotz and Loret has already taken us from history proper to prehistory twice. This alone, and not ethnography, brings us to the true primitives: thus its extreme importance for the problem of the origins of religion. Unfortunately, the data it provides are insufficient and partial, but even if they were still more limited, it would be imprudent to overlook them.

Excavations in caves dating from the Bronze Age and the Neolithic period have revealed human idols with neither arms nor legs, twin statues, birds, snakes, wheels, crosses, double crosses, and horses that are mythical symbols and prove, according to von Spiess, who has taken an inventory of them, the existence of a lunar mythology. In the southern Oran and Atlas, rock engravings of helmeted sheep and armored oxen urinating or receiving rain and of men playing ball before feathered animals can be compared with the South African rock carvings studied by Frobenius. This comparison reveals that in lands where drought is painfully present there is also a mimetic magic intended to call forth the water needed for life (Joleaud).

Especially since the discovery of the Chapelle-aux-Saints man, there is evidence that in the Paleolithic era there were man-made burial pits, stone protection for corpses, bones painted red, skeletons placed in the fetal position, and funerary meals. This indicates that in those far-off times there was a belief at least in survival after death and even in the effectiveness of piacular rites. However, Mainage refuses to confuse these simple rites with organized ancestor worship. Quaternary man painted animals, open hands, and masked dancers on the walls of caves, and since these paintings are always found in isolated, difficult to reach places, it seems unquestionable that they were taboo. Yet Reinach wanted to see them as new evidence of the primitiveness of totemism. There is no support for this, since each clan has its own special totem, but we always find the same animals everywhere at the same prehistoric level. The number of types of animal is very limited and seem to belong to fauna prior to that of the painters, who simply reproduced traditional images. Yet these paintings clearly prove that there was magic associated with hunting. Dancers wearing animal masks tried to reproduce animals' habits in order to ensure the multiplication of the species, and drawings of animals carrying the marks of blows were intended to facilitate, through mimesis, the success of hunting parties. Prehistory thus takes us back to the first outlines of mythology, magic, and ancestor worship. Of course, the religious representations themselves escape us since there are no written documents. We are thus thrown from prehistory to ethnography. Indeed, there are, or there were a few years ago, people whose material civilization is still in the Stone Age. Perhaps they could provide us with the solution to the mystery of origins? Since their civilization has not progressed, there are chances the same could be true of their religion.

However, a preliminary note is required. These savages have a past that is just as long as ours. Consequently, it would be curious to find that they had changed nothing over the ages and that their religion was exactly as it had been long ago. We can describe the present state of their religious systems, but nothing authorizes us to assert that theirs is indeed that of the primitive state, because the myths of these peoples often refer to a previous organization, for example, the Australian myths gathered by Van Gennep at a time when the matrimonial system was governed by different rules. However, ethnology, especially insofar as it sheds light on or confirms history and prehistory, is a precious source of information that we should use.

For far too long, sociologists have made the mistake of grouping under the generic name "primitives" both the non- and half-civilized black Africans, Oceanians, and American Indians. In fact, these peoples represent successive layers of civilization, from the Stone Age to the Iron Age. Animism, ancestor worship, and naturism stand side by side, and we cannot ascertain which came first. Now we are trying to find out which of these so-called primitives is the most backward, with the underlying idea that this will show us, if not the original religion, then at least the religion closest to the origin. Unfortunately, ethnologists have not come to an agreement on which people is the most primitive. Some hold that it is the Central

Australians, others that it is the Pygmies. Thus we have the debate between totemism and the religion of great gods.

The word *totem* is borrowed from the language of American Indians. However, American totemism is already highly evolved and so, generally, is that of the Australians, which is used to define this type of social system. The main elements are as follows:

1. Clans take the name of a specific object or being, preferably an animal, sometimes a plant, and occasionally a star or something else.

2. Members of the clan consider themselves to be related to the totem, which is generally seen as the first ancestor of the clan, and therefore, those who have the same totem are all related. Thus kinship is mystical and not related to blood.

3. The totem is taboo for the group that carries its name and cannot be killed or eaten; for example, a clan of the kangaroo totem would not be allowed to hunt or eat kangaroos.

4. Whether or not exogamy has another origin, in the vast majority of cases it is linked with totemism. A tribe is divided into two phratries, each with a different totem; for example, the two phratries of the Gournaditch-Mara have, respectively, white and black cockatoos as their totems. A woman from one phratry can marry only a man belonging to the other.

In addition to clan totemism, which is transmitted from generation to generation, there is sexual totemism, in which a totem is shared by all the women or all the men of a clan, and individual totemism, in which each person has his or her personal totem.

Frazer gave a series of three explanations of totemism. In *The Golden Bough* he likens it to the belief, so common among the noncivilized, in the existence of an exterior soul that can, like a material object, be removed from the individual to be stored for safekeeping in a secret place. In this way, sorcerers cannot steal it to harm the person. The tribes of central Australia carve the totem of a new-born child on a piece of wood called a *churinga*, which is kept in a secret, taboo place under the noble guard of the chief of the clan. If the *churinga* is lost or stolen, there is real mourning. Would this not be precisely because it in-carnated the soul of the child? The economic thesis that Frazer defended next, and that has often been put forth since, is based on the fact that Australian aborigines live in a desert and are perpetually haunted by the specter of famine. This explains the necessity of not killing animals or destroying edible plants so that the species does not disappear. These are totemic taboos. Frazer finally argued for the thesis of conception. He considered the Arunta to be the most primitive of all peoples because they are not aware of the physical process of conception. They think that the child enters into the woman when she first feels the fetus move. There could be nothing more natural than to identify the child with what struck the imagination of the mother at that time, such as a kangaroo running away or a snake slipping through the grass. This leads to the idea that the ancestor who is reincarnated in the child was haunting the place where the woman felt the first movement of the fetus and thus lived in the kangaroo or snake until it entered the mother. The child will thus take the animal's name, consider it to be a relative, and neither kill nor eat it. However, Mauss notes, against Spencer and Gillen, who also place them at the lowest level of humanity, that the Arunta are the only Australians to attribute totemic filiation to chance circumstances, whereas it is carefully determined everywhere else. Far from being the primitive form, the Arunta's totemism is a derived, decadent form. Thus we must look elsewhere.

American ethnologists consider the clan totem to be derived from the individual totem, which was initially a sort of protective spirit or guardian. This is the individualist theory. However, because American totemism is much more evolved than that of the Australians, it cannot provide the key to the latter. Saintyves links the system to the idea of mana, with the totem as the "benign form in which all the cosmic powers of the territory are concentrated." Van Gennep notes that, while this thesis can be argued for North American Indians, it cannot be transposed elsewhere. Pikler and Sombo have argued for a pictographic theory according to which the totem's origin is the drawing in which clan members use a type of animal or plant as a sign of recognition or rallying, for example, tattoos and emblems. Other tribes adopt the habit of thinking of the animal or plant at the same time as the clan, until they gradually become merged and identified with each other. Lang says that this theory makes the mistake of beginning with the image instead of simply the name, for the name necessarily preceded the image. Haddon and Schmidt have developed the regionalist and trade-based thesis. Animals live in herds, plants of the same species grow next to each other and the groups that live in the same regions as these animals and plants use them to trade for other foods they need. This form of commercial specialization gradually leads the buyers to identify the clan with the plant or animal that it trades.

Durkheim's theory will hold our attention a little longer. The other authors see totemism simply as a form of material organization or derive it from mana or the palingenesis presupposed by ancestor worship. In all these cases, totemism is not seen as the initial form of religious life. For Durkheim, on the contrary, totemic beliefs are of a manifestly religious nature since they involve a classification of things into the sacred and the secular:

> [W]e are assured that this religion is the most primitive one that is now observable and even, in all probability, that has ever existed. In fact, it is inseparable from a social organization on a clan basis. Not only is it impossible, as we have already pointed out, to define it except in connection with the clan, but it even seems as though the clan could not exist in the form it has taken in a great number of Australian societies, without the totem. For the members of a single clan are not united to each other by a common habitat or by common blood, as they are not necessarily consanguineous and are frequently scattered over different parts of the tribal territory. Their unity comes solely from their having the same name and the same emblem, . . . their participating in the same totemic cult. (Durkheim, 1915, 167 [1912, 238–39])

Like Lang, Durkheim defends a nominalist theory of totemism. In its primitive form, the totem is only the name, emblem, or symbol of the clan, a means by which the members of the group can recognize each other and feel solidarity with one another. While Lang stops at nominalism, Durkheim goes beyond it to assert that when the totem is worshiped, it is actually the clan itself that is addressed, through the intermediary of the totem. Society is the god. Thus we come back to the thesis previously analyzed, which sees religious feeling as a simple hypostasis of social feeling, a deification of the community.

Does totemism really substantiate this conclusion? Durkheim could allow himself to see totemism as the deification of society if the totem were a god or at least if it were worshiped as a god. However, it is simply the object of familial respect, similar to that of the son for his father, and not an object of mystical fear. Thus, totemism requires an explanation other than that of "collectivism."[1] Indeed, is there proof for the claim by the head of French sociology that totemism is prior to all other cultural forms? Spencer and Gillen, who are very familiar with the Australian tribes since they were even initiated into their ceremonies, tell of the importance in these tribes of funeral rites, such as those of the Urpmilchima, which extend even to a simulated human sacrifice to the dead person. Durkheim took these facts into account and devoted a chapter of *The Elementary Forms of Religious Life* to what he calls piacular rites. However, he thinks these rites can be explained only by a lessening of the collective feeling and not by a belief in spirits. Here he departs from the Australian documents, which speak of the spirits of the dead, the Iruntarinia. These spirits are not totems that have received a promotion, for they never take the form of evolved animals or plants but always appear as "human beings who appear young, with no facial hair and slim, dark bodies." Thus, that totemism precedes animism is only a hypothesis. Australia provides us with no key to the problem of the origin of religion. Moreover, even if totemism did tell us something about the beginnings of religious feeling in Australia, this would not help much, for, as Mauss said in 1900, "totemism, in its well-defined forms, is found only in a limited geographical area and its universality is far from demonstrated."

But could there not be people from a civilization even more isolated than that of the Australians? Catholic sociologists think so. They believe that Pygmy civilization is the most ancient. Pygmies live by gathering and have very rudimentary tools made of wood and bone. They do not even know how to shape stone. While their animism, magic, and mythology are rudimentary, the Pygmies do believe in a great god. "The belief in a supreme Being and the way he is worshiped is the most noticeable feature of Pygmy religion. This supreme Being appears everywhere as the Creator and Sovereign Lord of the world." This leads to the conclusion that humanity's most primitive religion is monotheism but that it has constantly been degenerating (except, perhaps, among the Hebrews).

Unfortunately, the testimonies on which Schmidt bases his theory are contradicted by others. According to Lowie, the observers do not agree, and thus the evidence in favor of primitive monotheism remains "insufficient." In particular, the Pygmies of Africa are so fearful that virtually no precise knowledge can be obtained of their religion. Of course, we must not overlook the fact that there is a belief in great gods and that this notion is important, but, like totemism, the belief in these great gods is always related to animism, and it is impossible to demonstrate which of these religious beliefs predates the other. Finally, note that the Pygmies were forced out of their original habitats by stronger peoples. This probably caused a social crisis and a subsequent disorganization of their religious systems. Thus it is possible, as Mauss notes, that the great god is only a degenerate form of a prior concept, especially since it is often linked to the bipartite division of the society and recognized only by men or only by women.

Thus, history and ethnography can indeed take us from modern to more archaic forms of religious feeling, but it is impossible to reach the absolute beginning, the very origin of this sentiment. As far back as we can go, we will find forms that are already complex and in which beliefs of various types and, perhaps, various origins overlap.

CHAPTER 13

The Laws of the Evolution of Religion

The origins of religious feeling inevitably remain very obscure. Will we now have less difficulty tracing the evolution of human religion from this mysterious X? Will it now be easier to determine whether this evolution was the chance result of unpredictable and disorderly circumstances or subject to determinism and laws?

Many thinkers believe in the existence of these laws. However, not all begin from the same principles when they set out to discover them. Some look to psychology, others to sociology.

Freud is among the former. From his psychoanalytic research and observation of patients, he drew the following law regarding sexual life: the child begins in an autoerotic stage in which the focus of sexual tendencies is the individual's own body. This progresses to the phase in which an object is chosen. Between these two there is narcissism, in which the tendencies, initially independent of each other, are united but not yet directed to an outside object and remain focused on the self. Humanity's religious evolution would be analogous. "The animist phase corresponds to narcissism and the religious phase to that of objectivization, characterized by the fixation of the libido on the parents." The first form of organized religion would be totemism, in which the son's hatred of his father, the ravisher and possessor of women, is repressed by paternal authority and gives rise to the symbolism of the totem. The totem represents the father, is taboo, and yet is ritually killed during the *Intichiuma*. Finally, "the scientific phase has its counterpart in the individual's mature state, which is characterized by renunciation of the search for pleasure and subordination of the choice of an outside object to the conventions and requirements of society."

This theory rests on a postulate: the laws of health are the same as the laws of sickness. In order to trace the contours of the sexual evolution of the child, like those of humanity's religious evolution, Freud began with clinical data, observations of people who were ill. Personally, we do not think that it is possible to conclude from the pathological to the normal. To do so would risk producing veritable fictions, such as the explanation of totemism via the Oedipus complex, which is based on no real documentation since everything is postulated: totemism being preceded by a system in which the sons killed their fathers to steal their women, the identification of obsessive zoophobia with the animal symbolism of the hated father, and so on.

De la Grasserie also begins with psychology when, in *De la psychologie des religions*, he sees the following laws at play in the history of religion:

1. The law of effective causes and final causes. Just as man first allows himself to be led by his needs and then directs himself in accordance with his will, so religious phenomena are first explained by purely mechanical causes and then by intentional causes.

2. The law of condensation and rarefaction. There is
   a rhythm to psychic life requiring that a period of
   attention always be followed by a period of rest.
   Similarly, in the history of religion, periods of
   fervor are followed by periods of relaxation, and
   the concentration of priestly powers is followed by
   periods when they are broken up.

3. The law of alternation of the subjective and the
   objective, which states that religion begins with
   the worship of the self (the cult of the living person
   and of the dead), continues with the worship of
   external objects (naturism and polytheism), to result,
   through the confluence of the objective and the
   subjective, in animism, which probably accounts for
   external objects, but attributes to them souls that are
   the sole focus of worship.

Each of these laws could be criticized separately on
the basis of historical and ethnographical data. We will
simply say, very generally, that while psychology can in-
form us of the nature of religious feeling, it can teach us
nothing about its development, because that takes place
over time and sociology holds the title to this field. This
is what Cournot seems to have seen when, in his *Traité de
l'enchaînement des idées fondamentales*, he distinguishes religious instinct from the ideas through which it is expressed.
Religions can be born or die, or be replaced by other religions, but what is born or dies in this way is only a system
of ideas, dogmas, and myths. The religious instinct that
gave rise to them is innate in humans and always persists,

building new forms on the remains of the old. Psychology tries to explain this instinct, but sociology focuses on the changes in the systems of ideas to which it gives rise.

As noted in the introduction, from its beginning sociology has tried to solve the problem of the evolution of religious systems (for example, Comte's Law of Three Stages). At the beginning of humanity, in fetishism, "theological ideas adhere completely and directly to sensations themselves"; polytheism is an "initial general waning" of religious thought; and monotheism is an even greater one: "Catholicism remains constantly concerned, in real, personal, and collective life, with gradually increasing the usual field of human wisdom at the expense of divine inspiration." By a curious paradox, Protestantism, which claimed to return to precisely that divine inspiration, leads, through the room it accords free inquiry, to the definitive breakup of mystical representations. Thus, the law of evolution would be in the end the elimination of religious conceptions of the world. However, in the second part of his life, Comte was forced to recognize the primacy of the heart and the need to satisfy it. He was therefore led to create, as a substitute for revealed religion, "positive religion," or the worship of great men and humanity.

Durkheim adopted the thought of sociology's founder in *La Division du travail*, for example, when he says:

> In the beginning, everything is encompassed [by religion]: everything social is religious; the two words are synonymous. Then, little by little, the economic, political, and scientific functions break away from the religious

function. . . . Free thought does not date from our days or from 1789, the Reformation, Scholasticism, the fall of Greco-Roman polytheism, or oriental theocracies. It is a phenomenon that begins nowhere but that has constantly developed throughout all of history.

Further on he defines the evolution of religion as a "regression." Reinach revealed himself as a disciple of Durkheim when he described primitives as feeling that they were surrounded by formidable powers, living in perpetual fear. By regulating the number of taboos and claiming to be the only mediator between man and god, the priesthood classified these fears and reduced their number. In antiquity, religious activity was assigned days and times, thus leaving the individual greater freedom. By providing a rigid dogma, Christianity hastened the hour of liberation because, according to Reinach, once Christians have accepted the dogmas, they can engage in secular activities. The intellectual tyranny of Catholicism is thus a step toward freeing the soul, which remains the end toward which present civilization is moving.

These sociologists seem to us to have confused two entirely different phenomena: dissolution, that is, regression, and the differentiation of functions that were merged in the primitive state. Differentiation is indeed the law of evolution of religion, but it has nothing in common with regression. Religion loses in terms of extension, since it abandons fields where it has no reason to be, but what it loses in surface it gains in depth. Certainly it did play a considerable role among primitives, but only because it was merged with other elements, such as the economy, politics, and the family. Thus, the river bed was broad but the waters were full of impurities. The great law of the sociology of religion is not a walk toward death but, on the contrary, a movement toward the autonomy of the mystical function.

If there is a basis for our interpretation, could we not speak of progress in religion? This is Sabatier's opinion. He discovers this progress in the institutions that are continually spreading from the tribe, through the nation, to humanity as a whole in ideas that go from the crudest anthropomorphism to moral monotheism. He sees it in religion, as it breaks free of the constraints of magic and the self-interested contracts between humans and gods, to enable belief to soar up to the heavenly Father.

However, such theories leave out an important element of religion: its faithfulness to the past and its hatred of change. Bronze and Iron Age civilizations, for example, always use instruments dating from the Stone Age in their religions: the throats of sacrificial victims are cut with a shaped or polished flint. The formulas used in the past are conserved even when their meaning is no longer understood, and they are, for those who repeat them, true enigmas. Modern religion presents similar facts. The Catholic mass retains the formula "per quem haec omnia, Domine, semper bona creas, sanctificas...,"[1] which is wholly understandable when we remember that, though the formula corresponds to nothing today, in the ancient church grain, fruit, and wine were placed on the altar to be consecrated. These facts explain Vernes's opposition to the evolutionary thesis.

According to him, researchers could have imagined the idea of religious progress only by confusing official religion, the work of the educated priesthood, with true religion. The ancient barbarian cults survive in the latter. Polytheism has remained deeply imprinted with fetishism, as is seen in the gods of grottos, springs, and sacred trees. Fetishism and polytheism also remain in monotheism, in the form of the worship of saints and images. Thus Comte's three stages, far from succeeding one another, are simultaneous and interwoven.

Vernes's thesis is most solid with respect to the existence of remnants of religion. However, when these remnants no longer meet any need and have been maintained for some time, they still finally disappear, as we have seen in the case of Mannhardt's agrarian rituals, particularly since the war.

Between these two opposing theses, one of progress and the other of immobility, there is room for an intermediate solution that Reinach defended in his conference "Le Progrès en Réligion." Since religion believes it holds absolute truth, it considers it important that no changes be made to what the ancients taught. Thus it "cannot change per se. Far from evolving under its own spontaneous power, it is immobile in essence and mobile by accident." The question must now be asked: What factors cause these changes? Since people belong to both a religion and a specific social milieu, any modification in the latter would necessarily cause parallel changes in the former:

> In general, left to itself, [religion] would have no reason to change, but it is precisely not left to itself. The same people who fight, judge, deliberate and observe the regular movements of the stars for the sake of their herds and harvests today will tomorrow participate in the rituals of

religion as priests or believers, affirming their faith through their prayers and cementing it through sacrifices. We must accept the fact that the discoveries they make in the secular world do affect elements of the same nature that are included in the sacred order.

This is how religion can progress, by harmonizing with "profane progress."

This solution thus leads us to seek the laws of the evolution of religion in sociology and history. This is the method adopted by Hubert, who proposes four laws:

1. The law of syncretism, according to which "religions develop through gradual synthesis corresponding to the growing unification of groups that they link spiritually."

2. The law of integration, according to which religions incorporate ancient beliefs and religions, instead of completely destroying them.

3. The law of personification, which takes us from impersonal *mana* to personified gods and from vague deities, such as the Roman *Indigitamenta*, to well-defined gods.

4. The law of moral spiritualization, which would arise out of the introduction of ethical concerns into religious representations.

We need only list these laws to see that while they apply relatively well in the West (aside from the passage from mana to god, which we have already criticized), they impose too unidirectional a path on the various human groups. We have seen that we should think instead of a treelike evolution with divergent lines and, moreover, that if the laws of the evolution of religion are to be made even slightly more precise, they must be situated in time and space.

The word *evolutionary* itself can be misleading, for in everyday language *evolution* is in opposition to *revolution*. However, humanity's religious path does not at all follow in the footsteps of changes in social structure. Very often its tendency to split, as noted in chapter 6, causes it to form small societies of saints who become separate from the world and live jealously outside it, though such isolation cannot last. As Chevalier says, from time to time the clock has to be reset and a little push in the right direction is needed to adapt the mystical society to the general trend of secular life. The helping hands are in the form of the religious revolutions we call "awakenings." Chevalier writes, "The history of Protestant sects is a succession of awakenings, in other words, of immobile, rigid forms adjusting via coup d'états to the uninterrupted movement of history."

The conclusion we can draw from this is that our idea of humanity's religious evolution should not be too simplistic and we should not think of it as a continuous wave going in a single, well-defined direction. Since, in addition to sociological factors, which are the only ones we have discussed, other biological, psychological, and moral factors are still at play, the reader's impression of complexity can only grow. We do not intend to dispel this feeling.

Conclusion

Sociology of religion asserts that religious life is not exclusively mental and interior, but incarnated in a material body, the Church, in rituals and in ideas that can be called collective, which simply means that they are shared by a given group. Insofar as they are social, these institutions, ceremonies, and myths are subject to a degree of determinism that it is the task of sociology of religion to describe. This is what we have tried to do in the preceding pages.

However, we would like to end with two more remarks. First, we must not convert this description into an explanation of religion and, under the pretext that the facts of religion are related to social structure, see religion simply as a hypostasis of society. This position is clearly defensible, but just as clearly debatable. Thus proposing it would be a departure from pure positive science, which is what we have tried to avoid.

Second, the reason we have taken a strictly deterministic approach to religious facts is simply because in science there is only necessity. Sociology can therefore be constructed only if what is necessary can be approached using our means of investigation. However, if, in addition to collective trends and social needs, religion translates the solitary soliloquies of the soul, the secret stirring of the heart, and the nostalgia of the mind seeking the absolute,

then determinism will be permeated by unpredictable beginnings, mysterious seeds, and promises of unfamiliar
flowers. The sociology of religion can observe their presence, but it cannot explain them.

Notes

Introduction

1. [In general, Bastide provided few clues to the works he quoted in this book. He never included page numbers, often did not indicate the work, and sometimes did not mention the author. When I was able to locate the relevant passage in the source text, I noted the page number and work. However, time constraints made it impossible to locate the sources of many quotations. In these cases, I translated the passages myself and used Bastide's method of reference.—*Trans.*]

2. Magic

1. Luquet's work provides a historical confirmation of our point of view. He shows that the drawings of Paleolithic man reveal characteristics that are clearly magical only relatively late, beginning in the Solutrean culture.

3. Representational Elements

1. Regarding the meaning of shared representations, see note 2. [In the manner of Émile Durkheim, Bastide refers to the presence of collective life in the thinking and activity of individuals as *representations.*—*Trans.*]

2. In other words, but with no greater meaning, they are common to members of a collectivity, but no soul at all is attributed to them.

10. Relations among Religious Systems and Other Social Systems

1. There is, however, totemism where fishing is difficult (Descamps).

12. Historical and Ethnographic Data

1. In this chapter we do not intend to study totemism in itself. We have simply considered the claim that it is the original religion of humanity, which is why we have left aside a number of theories. Once its anteriority has been rejected, we need not find an explanation for it. However, if we were to seek one, my preference would be for a synthetic theory, such as those of Loisy and Van Gennep, or for theories of breakup, such as that of Descamps, or for Goldenweiser's so-called convergence theory. Indeed, these three theories are not mutually exclusive.

13. The Laws of the Evolution of Religion

1. ["through whom all these things, Lord, you always make good, sanctify..."—*Trans.*]

Bibliography

It would be impossible to provide a complete bibliography of the sociology of religion. For works published between 1896 and 1924 (with the interruption during the war), we refer the reader to that remarkable bibliographical tool, *Année sociologique* (Paris: Alcan). We limit this bibliography to those works cited in the text and other selected publications that offer a useful complement.

[*Unfortunately, not all of the works and authors cited in the text are listed here. When I was able to find the work cited, I added it to Bastide's list, but I did not add the name of authors whose works I was unable to identify.*—Trans.]

Allen, G. 1897. *The Evolution of the Idea of God.* London.

Allier, R. 1927. *Le Non-civilisé et nous.* Paris: Payot.

———. 1927. *La Psychologie de la conversion chez les peuples non civilisés.* Paris: Payot.

Belot. 1909. *Religion et morale.* Paris: Alcan.

Bérard, V. 1894. *De l'origine des cultes arcadiens.* Thorin.

Bergson, H. 1935 [1932]. *The Two Sources of Morality and Religion.* Translated by R. Ashley Audra and Cloudesly Bereton. New York: Holt. Originally published as *Les Deux Sources de la morale et de la religion* (Paris: Alcan).

Bouché-Leclerc, A. 1879–82. *Histoire de la divination dans l'antiquité.* 4 vols. Paris.

Bros, A. 1907. *Religions des peuples non civilisés.* Paris.

Chevalier, J. *Essai sur la formation de la nationalité et les réveils religieux au Pays de Galles.* A. de l'U. de Lyon, N.S. no. 34.

Codrington, R. H. 1891. *The Melanesians.* Oxford: Clarendon Press.

Comte, A. 1905 [1835–52]. *The Fundamental Principles of the Positive Philosophy.* Translated by Paul Descours and H. Gordon Jones. London: Watts. Originally published as *Cours de philosophie positive* (Paris: Borrani et Droz).

Czarnowski. 1919. *Saint Patrick*. Paris: Alcan.

Davies, T. W. 1897. *Magic, Divination and Demonology*. London: Clarke.

Decharme, P. 1886. *Mythologie de la Grèce antique*. Garnier.

Deffontaines. 1934. *Introduction à une géographie des religions*. Chronique sociale.

Delacroix, H. 1922. *La Religion et la foi*. Paris: Alcan.

Descamps, P. 1929. "Les Origines du totémisme collectif." *Revue internationale de sociologie* 37, nos. 3–4.

Dieterich, A. 1905. *Mutter Erde*. Leipzig.

Doutté, F. 1909. *Magie et religion dans l'Afrique du Nord*. Jourdan, Algiers.

Dumézil, G. 1924. *Le Festin d'immortalité*. Geuthner.

Durkheim, É. 1915 [1912]. *The Elementary Forms of Religious Life*. Translated by Joseph Ward Swain. New York: Free Press. Originally published as *Les formes élémentaires de la vie religieuse* (Paris: Alcan).

Dussaud, R. 1914. *Introduction à l'histoire des religions*. Leroux.

Ehrenreich, P. 1910. *Die allgemeine Mythologie*. Leipzig.

Favre, B. 1932. *Les Sociétés secrètes en Chine*. Maisonneuve.

Fossey, C. 1902. *La Magie assyrienne*. Leroux.

Foucart, J. 1912. *Histoire des religions et méthode comparative*. Picard.

Frazer, J. G. 1910. *Totemism and Exogamy*. London: Macmillan.

———. 1913 *The Scapegoat*.

———. 1920 *The Magical Origin of Kings*.

———. 1957 [1922]. *The Golden Bough*. 1 vol. Abridged ed. New York: Macmillan.

Freud, S. 1918 [1912]. *Totem and Taboo*. Translated by A. A. Brill. New York: Moffat, Yard and Co. Originally published as *Totem und Tabu* (Leipzig: Hugo Heller).

Frobenius. 1898. *Die Masken und Geheimbünde Afrikas*. (Cited in Trilles 1912, *Le Totémisme chez les Fân*. Bibliothèque Anthropos.)

Fustel de Coulanges. 1881. *La Cité antique*. Hachette.

Gasquet. 1899. *Essai sur le culte et les mystères de Mithra*. Colin.

Gernet, L., and A. Boulanger. *Le Génie grec dans la religion*. Paris: Renaissance du livre, B.S.H. no. 11.

Goblet d'Alviella. 1911. *Croyances, rites, institutions*. 3 vols. Geuthner.

Goguel. 1926 [1925]. *Jesus the Nazarene: Myth or History*. Translated by Frederick Stephens. London: Fisher Unwin. Originally published as *Jésus de Nazareth: Mythe ou histoire* (Payot).

Granet, M. 1958 [1929]. *Chinese Civilization*. Translated by Kathleen E. Innes and Mabel R. Brailsford. New York: Meridian Books. Originally published as *La Civilisation chinoise* (Paris: Renaissance du livre).

Grasserie, de la, R. 1899. *De la psychologie des religions*. Paris: Alcan.

———. 1899. *Des religions comparées au point de vue sociologique*. Giard.

Guignebert. 1910. *L'Évolution des dogmes*. Flammarion.

———. 1929. *Le Christianisme*. Flammarion.

———. *Jésus*. Paris: Renaissance du livre, B.S.H. no. 29.

Guyau. 1902. *L'Irreligion de l'avenir*. Paris: Alcan.

Henry, V. 1914. *La Magie dans l'Inde antique*. Dujarric.

Hertz, R. 1928. *Mélanges de sociologie religieuse et folklore*. Paris: Alcan.

Hewitt, J. N. B. 1910. *Orenda*. Washington.

Hubert, H. 1904. *Préface du Manuel d'histoire des religions de Chantepie de la Saussaye*. French translation, Armand Colin.

Hubert, H., and M. Mauss. 1902. *Esquisse d'une théorie générale de la magie*. Année sociologique.

———. 1909. *Mélanges d'histoire des religions*. Paris: Alcan.

Huvelin, P. *Magie et droit individual*. Année sociologique, X.

Jevons, J. B. 1896. *Introduction to the History of Religion*. London.

King, J. H. 1892. *The Supernatural*. London.

Lagrange, M. J. 1903. *Études sur les religions sémitiques*. Paris.

Lang, A. 1899. *The Making of Religion*. London: Longmans, Green and Company, Ltd.

Larock, V. 1932. *Essai sur la valeur sacrée des noms de personnes*. Leroux.

Laveleye, de, E. 1875. *Le Protestantisme et le catholicisme dans leurs rapports avec la liberté et la prospérité des peuples*. Rev. de Belgique.

Le Coeur, C. 1932. *Le Culte de la génération et l'évolution religieuse et sociale en Guinée*. Leroux.

Lehmann, F. R. 1915. *Mana*. Leipzig.

Le Roy, E. 1911. *La Religion des primitifs*. 3rd ed. Beauchesne.

Leroy, O. 1927. *La Raison primitive*. Geuthner.

Lessmann, H. 1908. *Aufgaben und Ziele der vergleichenden Mythenforschung*. Leipzig.

Lévy-Bruhl, L. 1923 [1922]. *Primitive Mentality*. Translated by Lilian A. Claire. New York: Macmillan. Originally published as *La Mentalité primitive* (Paris: Alcan).

―――. 1926 [1910]. *How Natives Think.* Translated by Lilian A. Claire. London: Allen and Unwin. Originally published as *Les Fonctions mentales dans les sociétés inférieures* (Paris: Alcan).

―――. 1928 [1927]. *The "Soul" of the Primitive.* Translated by Lilian A. Claire. New York: Macmillan. Originally published as *L'Âme primitive* (Paris: Alcan).

―――. 1935. *La Mythologie primitive.* Paris: Alcan.

―――. 1936 [1931]. *Primitives and the Supernatural.* Translated by Lilian A. Claire. London: Allen and Unwin. Originally published as *Le Surnatural et la nature dans la mentalité primitive* (Paris: Alcan).

Lods, A. 1906. *La Croyance en la vie future et le culte des morts dans l'antiquité israélite.* 2 vols. Fischbacher.

―――. *Israël.* Paris: Renaissance du livre, B.S.H. no. 27.

Loisy. 1914. *Le Régime du sacrifice dans les différentes religions.* Rev. Bleue.

―――. 1914. *Les Mystères païens et le mystère chrétien.* Nourry.

―――. 1920. *Essai historique sur le sacrifice.* Nourry.

Loret. 1906. *L'Égypte au temps du totémisme.* Conf. Guimet.

Lowie, R. 1924. *Primitive Religion.* New York: Liveright.

Lubbock, J. 1870. *The Origin of Civilization and the Primitive Condition of Man.* New York: Appleton.

Mainage. 1924. *Les Religions de la préhistoire.* Paris: Desclée.

Mannhardt. 1875. *Wald und Feldkulte.* 2 vols. Berlin.

Marett, R. R. 1900. *Preanimistic Religion.* Folklore.

Marillier, L. 1894. *La Survivance de l'âme et l'idée de justice chez les peuples non civilisés.* École des Hautes Études.

―――. 1901. "Note sur la coutume, le tabou et l'obligation morale." In *Entre camarades.* Paris: Alcan.

Mauss, M. 1979 [1904–5]. *Seasonal Variations of the Eskimo.* Translated by James J. Fox. London: Routledge and Kegan Paul. Originally published as *Essai sur les variations saisonnières dans les sociétés eskimos* (Année sociologique, IX).

Meinhoff. 1926. *Die Religionen der Afrikaner.* Oslo.

Moret, A. 1908. *Au temps des Pharaons.* Colin.

―――. 1911. *Rois et dieux d'Égypte.* Colin.

―――. 1913. *Mystères égyptiens.* Colin.

Moret and Davy. *Des clans aux Empires.* Paris: Renaissance du livre, B.S.H. no. 6.

Müller, J. G. 1855. *Amerikanischen Urreligionen.* Basel.

Müller, M. 1879. *Essais sur l'histoire des religions*. French translation by Georges Harris. Didier.

Nieuwenhuis, A. W. 1917. *Die Wurzeln des Animismus*. Leiden.

Oldenberg, H. 1988 [1894]. *The Religion of the Veda*. Translated by Shridhor B. Shrotri. Delhi: Motilal Banarsidass. Originally published as *Die Religion des Veda* (Berlin).

Pinard de la Boullaye. 1922. *L'Étude comparée des religions*. 2 vols. Beauchesne.

Potter, M. A. 1902. *Sohrab and Rustem: The Epic Theme of a Combat between Father and Son*. London: Natt.

Preuss, S. *Ursprung der Religion und Kunst*. Globus, 86 and 87.

Reinach, K. T. 1904–5. *Mythes, cultes et religions*. 4 vols. Leroux.

Renan. 1887. *Histoire du peuple d'Israël*. 5 vols.

Rhode, E. 1891–94. *Psyché, Seelencult, und Unterblichkeitsglaube der Griechen*. Tübingen.

Richard, G. 1924. *L'Athéisme dogmatique en sociologie religieuse*. Strasbourg.

Robertson Smith, W. 1889. *The Religion of the Semites*. London.

Sabatier, A. 1897. *Esquisse d'une philosophie de la religion*. Paris.

Saintyves. 1907. *Les Saints, successeurs des dieux*. Nourry.

———. 1914. *La Force magique*. Nourry.

———. 1923. *Essais de folklore biblique*. Nourry.

Schmidt, W. 1926. *Ursprung der Gottesidee*. Münster.

———. 1931. *Origine et évolution de la religion*. French translation, Grasset.

Söderblom. 1916. *Das Werden des Gottersglaubens*. German translation, Leipzig.

Spencer, H. 1896. *Principles of Sociology*. New York: Appleton.

Spencer and Gillen. 1899. *The Native Tribes of Central Australia*. New York.

Spiess, von, K. 1910. *Prähistorie und Mythus*. Wiener-Neustadt.

Steinmetz. 1895. *Lohn und Strafe in Jenseits der Wilden*.

Tiele, C. P. 1899. *Einleitung in die Religionwissenschaft*. Gotha.

Toutain, F. 1909. *Études de mythologie et d'histoire des religions antiques*. Paris: Hachette.

Trilles, R. P. H. 1912. *Le Totémisme chez les Fân*. Bibliothèque Anthropos.

Tylor, E. B. 1891. *Primitive Culture*. London: Murray.

Usener, H. 1896. *Götternamen*. Bonn.

Van Gennep. 1904. *Tabou et totémisme à Madagascar*. Leroux.

———. 1910. *Formation des légendes*. Flammarion.

———. 1920. *État actuel du problème totémique*. Leroux.

———. 1960 [1909]. *The Rites of Passage*. Translated by Monika B. Vizedom and Gabrielle L. Caffe. Chicago: University of Chicago Press. Originally published as *Les Rites de passage* (Nourry).

Weber, M. 1920. *Gesammelte Aufsätze zur Religionssoziologie*. 3 vols. Tübingen.

Webster, H. 1908. *Primitive Secret Societies*. London.

Will, R. 1915. *Le Culte*. Strasbourg: T.I.

Wundt. 1910. *Völkerpsychologie: Mythus und Religion*. 2nd ed. 3 vols. Leipzig.

Index

Roger Bastide (1898–1974) was trained in philosophy, but his interests soon led him to anthropology and sociology. He replaced Claude Lévi-Strauss in São Paulo, Brazil; later became a professor at the École Pratique des Hautes Études in Paris; received the Légion d'honneur; and was awarded a chair at the Sorbonne. He wrote more than eight hundred articles and thirty books, including *The African Religions of Brazil*, *African Civilizations in the New World*, and *Applied Anthropology*.

Mary Baker is a professional translator with a background in philosophy. Among her translations are *Claude Lévi-Strauss and the Making of Structural Anthropology* by Marcel Hénaff (Minnesota, 1998) and *The Existence of the External World* by Jean-René Vernes.

James L. Peacock is the Distinguished Kenan Professor of Anthropology at the University of North Carolina at Chapel Hill.